THE POWER

OF

BELIEF

How Ideas Shape Leaders, Nations, and the Future

Mardoche Sidor, MD

Karen Dubin, PhD, LCSW

SWEET Institute

SWEET Institute Publishing

Transformational Books for a Transformational World.

Published by:

SWEET Institute Publishing

New York, NY

WWW.SWEETInstitutePublishing.com

First Edition

Printed in the United States of America

ISBN (Paperback): 978-1-968105-00-6

Cover Design: SWEET Institute Publishing

Interior Design and Layout: SWEET Institute Publishing

For bulk orders, permissions, or media inquiries, please contact:

info@sweetinstitutepublishing.com

SWEET Institute Publishing

Transformational Books for a Transformational World

Dedication

To those who dared to believe when no one else did.

To the ones who kept going when the world said stop.

To the quiet visionaries, the wounded healers, the resilient leaders, and the everyday people shaping the future through faith, conviction, and courage.

This book is for you.

Because belief, yours, is how the world changes.

Other Books

By Mardoche Sidor, M.D; Karen Dubin, PhD, LCSW; with the SWEET Institute

- Journey to Empowerment
- Discovering Your Worth: Everything You Need to Feel Fulfilled
- The Power of Faith: A Harvard-Trained Psychiatrist Speaking on Faith
- The Psychotherapy Certificate Course: The Clinician and Coach Manual (Books 1–3)
- The Anxiety Course: The Workbook
- What's Missing
- NLP for Clinicians

Table of Contents

Foreword

By Jacob M. Appel, M.D., J.D., M.P.H., MPhil.
Director of Ethics Education in Psychiatry, Mount Sinai Icahn School of Medicine

Belief is one of the most powerful and least understood forces in human affairs. It transcends culture, religion, and ideology. It underpins the rise and fall of empires, drives scientific discovery, and defines our collective sense of morality and purpose. And yet, for all its influence, belief often operates silently, invisibly, beneath the surface of our actions and institutions.

In The Power of Belief, the authors embark on an ambitious and much-needed exploration of how beliefs shape not only individual identity, but also leadership, institutions, and historical momentum. They invite us to reflect not only on what we believe, but on how we come to believe, and what that means for our role in shaping the world.

This is not a partisan book, nor is it an endorsement of any particular political figure. It is a study of belief as a psychological and sociological phenomenon. To that end, the authors take on the challenging task of examining the role of belief in the rise of controversial figures, including President Donald Trump. Their approach is clinical and analytical rather than polemical, offering the reader an opportunity to consider belief not as inherently good or bad, but as a tool with vast potential for both creation and destruction.

What makes this book particularly valuable is its balance of theory and application. The authors do not stop at describing the mechanics of belief; they offer practical frameworks for examining and transforming our own belief systems. They encourage the reader not simply to believe, but to believe intentionally, to align one's beliefs with one's values, purpose, and aspirations.

In a time when misinformation spreads quickly, polarization deepens, and certainty often replaces curiosity, a book like this is both urgent and hopeful. It reminds us that belief is not just something we hold, it's something we shape. And by shaping it, we shape the future.

I commend the authors for their bold and nuanced exploration of one of the most defining elements of human life. May this work serve as a catalyst for critical reflection, meaningful dialogue, and ultimately, intentional action.

Jacob M. Appel, M.D., J.D., M.P.H.; MPhil.

Director of Ethics Education in Psychiatry, & Associate Director, Academy for Medicine & the Humanities
Mount Sinai Icahn School of Medicine
Author, Who Says You're Dead? Medical & Ethical Dilemmas for the Curious & Concerned

Preface

By Jules Ranz, M.D.
Clinical Professor of Psychiatry, Columbia University Vagelos College of Physicians and Surgeons
Former Director, Columbia University Public Psychiatry Fellowship

In public psychiatry, we are often reminded that the most powerful forces shaping a person's life are not always visible. They are found not only in diagnostic categories or clinical interventions, but in a person's sense of possibility, agency, and meaning, in what they believe about themselves, others, and the world around them.

This book is a timely and ambitious effort to bring that truth to a broader audience. It offers a sweeping exploration of belief, not just as a personal or psychological phenomenon, but as a force that shapes leadership, movements, institutions, and ultimately, history.

The authors ask: What enables some individuals to mobilize millions, reshape systems, and persist in the face of adversity, while others with similar intelligence or skill remain unheard? Their answer: belief. Not belief as naïveté or ideology, but belief as conviction, clarity, and sustained internal alignment.

The book does not shy away from complexity. It begins by examining one of the most polarizing figures in contemporary history, Donald Trump, not to glorify or vilify, but to analyze. To understand how belief, when unshakable, can galvanize action on a massive scale, for better or worse. And perhaps more importantly, how that same dynamic can be used toward positive transformation, in clinical work, in leadership, and in our collective life.

What makes The Power of Belief particularly meaningful is that it moves beyond theory. The authors integrate insights from psychology, neuroscience, and history, but they also offer frameworks for personal reflection and social impact. They invite readers to examine the beliefs they've inherited, to question them thoughtfully, and to cultivate systems of belief that promote healing, growth, and meaningful action.

This book will resonate with clinicians, educators, activists, and anyone seeking to understand not only how the world works, but how it can be changed, starting from within. It does not offer easy answers. But it encourages something far more enduring: the willingness to ask better questions, to believe in our collective capacity for change, and to engage that belief in ways that matter.

It has been a pleasure to witness the evolution of this work, and I commend the authors for their clarity, courage, and vision.

Jules Ranz, M.D.

Clinical Professor of Psychiatry, Columbia University Vagelos College of Physicians and Surgeons
Former Director, Columbia University Public Psychiatry Fellowship

Introduction

The Power of Belief: An Introduction

Belief is not just a thought or an idea; it is a force—one that shapes our reality, drives our actions, and ultimately defines the trajectory of our lives. It is the lens through which we interpret the world, the foundation upon which we build our dreams, and the energy that propels us toward or away from our goals. Belief is both subtle and profound, an invisible yet unstoppable current that runs through every decision, every ambition, and every success.

In the simplest terms, belief is a powerful mental and emotional state that compels us to act. When we believe in something—whether it's a cause, an idea, or ourselves—we align our thoughts, energy, and actions toward that belief. It shapes what we see, how we perceive our challenges, and what we feel capable of achieving. It influences how we engage with others, how we react to setbacks, and how we envision the future.

But belief isn't always rational. It's not confined by logic or reason. In fact, some of the most extraordinary accomplishments in history have been driven by beliefs that, on the surface, may have seemed implausible or impossible. The belief that humans could fly led to the Wright brothers' invention of the airplane. The belief that change was possible propelled Martin Luther King Jr. to lead the civil rights movement. The belief that a small group of individuals could impact the fate of the world inspired countless revolutionaries, thinkers, and visionaries.

Belief has the power to create movements. It can unite people, ignite passion, and fuel collective action. It can give rise to revolutions and revolutions in thought. But perhaps most importantly, belief has the ability to shape the course of one's own life. When we believe in ourselves—when we cultivate a deep sense of inner confidence and trust in our abilities—we unlock our full potential. Belief becomes the catalyst for action, and action becomes the path to transformation.

This book explores the extraordinary power of belief—not only in shaping individual destinies but also in the collective impact we have on the world. We'll delve into the ways belief influences the leaders of our time, the way it drives mass movements, and how we can use belief to unlock our highest potential. Through a combination of case studies, psychological insights, and practical strategies, this book will show you how to harness the power of belief in your own life.

Throughout this journey, you'll learn that belief is not a passive force. It is an active practice—one that requires conscious cultivation and unwavering commitment. Beliefs are not static; they can evolve and grow. But to unlock their full potential, we must understand how they are formed, how they can be strengthened, and how we can use them as tools for transformation.

This book isn't just about understanding belief—it's about living it. It's about learning how to not only believe in yourself but to help others believe in themselves, and to build belief systems that empower you to take bold action in the world. Belief is the key to unlocking your greatest potential, and by the end of this book, you will have the tools to master it.

The power of belief is waiting to be unleashed. It's time to tap into that power and change the world—starting with your own life.

Why This Book?

In a world that often seems divided, chaotic, and uncertain, there is one universal force that has the potential to transcend boundaries, heal wounds, and create lasting change: Belief. Our beliefs shape our thoughts, our decisions, and our actions. They are the invisible threads that weave together the fabric of our reality, and they have the power to determine the course of our lives. Whether we are conscious of it or not, belief is the driving force behind everything we do.

This book was born out of a deep curiosity and a desire to understand how belief shapes the world around us. It was inspired by the realization that the most transformative leaders, visionaries, and change-makers throughout history have all shared one key trait: An unwavering belief in themselves, in their mission, and in the possibility of a better future.

But belief is not always easy. In a world filled with noise, distraction, and uncertainty, it's easy to lose sight of what we truly believe and allow doubt to take root. It's easy to be swayed by the opinions of others, to follow the status quo, and to settle for mediocrity. But the individuals who change the world are the ones who are willing to believe in the impossible, to push through the obstacles, and to stand firm in their vision—even when the world around them doubts them.

This book will help you unlock that power of belief. It is not about following someone else's dream or subscribing to someone else's vision. It's about discovering your own beliefs and understanding how they shape your actions and impact the world. We'll explore the psychology behind belief, the science of how beliefs are formed, and how they can be harnessed to create massive change in your own life and the lives of others.

We'll dive into the case study of Donald Trump, a figure whose belief in his own success has inspired millions and sparked fierce debate around the world. Regardless of your political views, Trump's ability to galvanize people and create a movement is a testament to the power of belief. He didn't just believe in his own success; he instilled that belief in others. His journey provides valuable lessons on how belief can become a catalyst for action, how it can spark movements, and how it can inspire others to rally behind a shared vision.

But this book isn't just about one person's journey. It's about you. It's about how you can build an unshakable belief system that empowers you to reach your fullest potential, whether in your career, your personal life, or your role as a leader. This book will guide you through the process of understanding and cultivating your own beliefs, helping you to tap into the power of belief to transform your life.

An Introduction by Robert Holden, PhD

Welcome to this gem of a book, *The Power of Belief*, written by my dear friend Mardoche Sidor. Inside these pages you will discover a whole new way to be in the world. *When you change your beliefs, you change your life.*

First, I would like to tell you a story.

Michael, a physician, came to see me with a bad case of insomnia. He was tired, gaunt, and had not slept a wink for several nights. "Something is keeping me up at night," he told me. When I asked him what medication he was on, he told me that he preferred not to take meds as they make him feel drowsy in the day.

That night, Michael reluctantly agreed to take one sleeping pill. He got into bed, turned off the light, and reached over for the pill on his bedside table. He swallowed it whole, closed his eyes, and the next thing he knew … it was morning. Michael had slept the whole night. He could hardly believe it. But what happened next was even more unbelievable.

As Michael threw off his bedsheets, he saw that the sleeping pill was still on the bedside table. What had happened? The pill was untouched, but Michael's pajama button was missing. "I must have swallowed the pyjama button in the belief it was the sleeping pill," he told me.

What helped Michael get a good night's sleep was not a magical pajama button; it was what the medical profession calls the healing power of *placebo*. The word "placebo" translated means *a pleasing belief*.

Beliefs are powerful. Mardoche knows this very well, both as a physician and a philosopher. That's why he called this book *The Power of Belief*.

As you read Mardoche's book, I invite you to examine your beliefs.

What beliefs help you to be expansive, creative, and to express yourself fully? Make a list of your most life affirming beliefs. Notice the beliefs that increase your sense of aliveness, open your heart, and help you achieve impossible things. Recognize the beliefs that give you faith, strength, and courage. Remember what Jesus said, "Believe in me, and you will do the works that I do; and greater works than these you will do," Gospel of John 14:12.

Notice also the limiting beliefs that hold you back. For example, pay attention to your cynicism. Cynicism is a crisis of faith. Cynicism hides an old wound. Cynicism is a defence against feeling hopeful. Ask yourself, *what beliefs that no longer work for me?* For example, do you suffer from what I call *dysfunctional independence?* Do you believe life loves you and that life has your back; or do you believe "I'm on my own" and "It's me against the world*?"* Do you believe asking for help is a weakness or a strength?

When you open your mind, and allow yourself to experience the power of belief, it will shift your psychology, and it will change the way you experience life. Moreover, you will a realm of inspiration in which you discover a power within you far greater than you imagine. This power belongs to what philosophers and mystics call your "I AM" which is the spirit and essence of your True Self.

May your beliefs give you wings. May you soar high. May you see each setback as an opportunity. May your thoughts be transformed from fear into love. Choose your beliefs carefully, and you will succeed at becoming yourself and at being a truly loving presence in the world.

Robert Holden, PhD

author of *Shift Happens!* and

Higher Purpose

Acknowledgments

This book is the result of many voices, countless conversations, and the enduring support of a community committed to growth, healing, and transformation.

To the clinicians, educators, leaders, and learners who make up the SWEET Institute family, thank you for showing us, time and again, the power of belief in action. Your courage, curiosity, and commitment to unlearning, relearning, and co-creating a better world have inspired every page of this work.

To our mentors and colleagues in psychiatry, psychology, and social work, especially those who have walked before us and alongside us, thank you for planting the seeds of inquiry, integrity, and hope. We are especially grateful to Dr. Jules Ranz, whose visionary leadership in public psychiatry has shaped generations of healers, and to Dr. Robert Holden, whose innovative work on psychology and spirituality has been featured on The Oprah Winfrey Show, Good Morning America, a PBS show called Shift Happens!.

To our families and loved ones—thank you for believing in us, even when the vision was unclear. Your patience, presence, and love have sustained us through early mornings, late nights, and the sacred process of bringing this message into form.

To those who challenge systems, speak truth, and imagine boldly, this book is for you. Your belief in something better is the light that keeps us moving forward.

And finally, to the reader: thank you for taking this journey with us. May this book serve not as a final word, but as an invitation, to reflect, to reimagine, and to remember that belief, when cultivated with intention and courage, can transform not only your life, but the world.

With deep gratitude,

Mardoche Sidor, M.D.
Karen Dubin, Ph.D., LCSW
SWEET Institute

PART I

Understanding the Nature of Belief

Chapter 1

What's In A Belief?

"A belief is not just an idea the mind possesses; it is an idea that possesses the mind." — Robert Oxton Bolton

The Statement That Shook the World

"I believe I was saved by God to make America great again." These words encapsulate a worldview, a purpose, and a mission. Whether you agree or disagree with Donald Trump, this belief has mobilized millions, shaped policies, sparked protests, and redefined modern politics. But beyond Trump, beyond politics—what makes a belief so powerful that it moves the world?

We often assume beliefs are personal, tucked away in the mind like books on a shelf. But beliefs don't just sit idle. They direct actions, dictate decisions, and determine destinies. They can build nations or burn them down. They can liberate people or enslave them. History has shown us that a single belief, held with conviction, is often more powerful than armies, wealth, or technology.

The Anatomy of Belief

A belief is more than a thought—it is a psychological force. To understand its power, let's break it down:

THE ANATOMY OF BELIEF

A BELIEF IS A LENS

It filters reality, shaping how we interpret the world

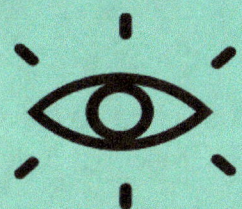

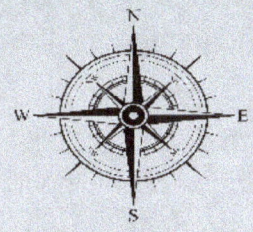

A BELIEF IS A COMPASS

It directs choices, actions, and strategies.

A BELIEF IS A MAGNET

It attracts like-minded people and repels those who challenge it.

A BELIEF IS AN ARMOR

It protects against doubt, criticism, and fear

Trump's statement is not just about faith or politics—it is about identity. To his supporters, it signals divine purpose, national revival, and unwavering leadership. To his critics, it represents delusion, dangerous populism, or authoritarianism. The same words, but radically different interpretations. This is the nature of belief—it divides and unites with equal force.

The Science Behind Belief

Neuroscience reveals that beliefs are wired deep in the brain.[1] The reticular activating system (RAS) acts as a filter, prioritizing information that aligns with existing beliefs while ignoring contradictions.[2] This is why political debates rarely change minds—beliefs are not just thoughts, they are neurological circuits reinforced by emotion.

Studies on confirmation bias show that once a belief takes root, the brain resists change.[3] This is why people cling to ideas even when confronted with facts. The stronger the emotional attachment, the harder it is to break.

So, what happens when a person believes they were chosen by God for a mission? History tells us: they become unstoppable. From Joan of Arc to Martin Luther King Jr., those who truly believe they have divine purpose move mountains.

---

[1] Cristofori, Irene, and Jordan Grafman. "Neural underpinnings of the human belief system." *Processes of Believing: The Acquisition, Maintenance, and Change in Creditions* (2017): 111-123.

[2] Sousa, David A. *How the brain learns*. Corwin Press, 2016.

[3] Viskontas, Indre. "The challenges of changing minds: How confirmation bias and pattern recognition affect our search for meaning." *Pseudoscience: The conspiracy against science* (2018): 451-463.

Belief as a Weapon and a Tool

Belief can create or destroy. Hitler believed in Aryan supremacy—millions died. Gandhi believed in nonviolence—millions were freed. The difference was not the strength of their belief, but the direction of it.

Trump's belief is not unique. Leaders throughout history have invoked divine purpose to rally people. Some have saved nations; others have led them to ruin. The question we must ask is: How do we harness belief for good?

Your Beliefs, Your Power

This book is not about Trump. It is about you.

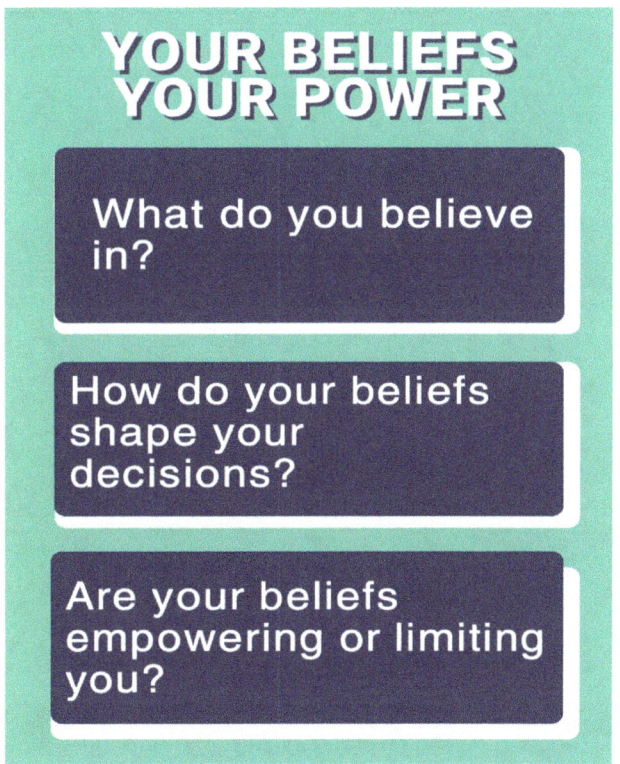

YOUR BELIEFS YOUR POWER

What do you believe in?

How do your beliefs shape your decisions?

Are your beliefs empowering or limiting you?

By the end of this journey, you will not only understand the psychology of belief, but you will master it. You will learn how to create, refine, and wield belief like the most powerful leaders in history. You will see how belief can transform your life, your work, and even the world.

So, the real questions are:

What do you believe? And what will you do with that belief?

Chapter 2

The Psychology of Belief

"Whether you think you can or you think you can't, you're right."
— Henry Ford

The Invisible Force That Shapes Everything

Imagine two people standing in the same storm. One sees it as a disaster, the other as a test of resilience. Same reality, different reactions—why? Belief.

Beliefs are the foundation of everything we do. They dictate whether we take risks or play it safe, fight for change or accept the status quo, build empires or live in fear. A belief is the difference between a person who sees themselves as a failure and one who sees themselves as destined for greatness.

Donald Trump believes he was chosen by God to make America great again. Whether you see that as arrogance, inspiration, or delusion, one thing is clear: This belief has shaped his actions, fueled his influence, and driven millions to follow him.

But what is a belief, really? And how does it become so powerful?

How Beliefs Are Formed

Beliefs are not facts. They are mental shortcuts—stories we tell ourselves to make sense of the world. But once a belief takes root, the brain treats it as truth.[4]

---

[4] Humpston, Clara S. "Understanding beliefs." (2015): 270-273.

The Three Pillars of Belief Formation:

1. **Repetition**: The more we hear something, the more we believe it. This is why propaganda, marketing, and slogans are effective. ("Make America Great Again." "Yes We Can.")
2. **Emotion**: Beliefs tied to strong emotions—fear, love, anger—are nearly unshakable.
3. **Authority**: If someone we trust or admire says it, we are more likely to believe it. (Religious leaders, politicians, parents, celebrities.)

These pillars explain why Trump's core supporters remain loyal despite scandals, legal battles, and controversies. They are not following a man—they are following a belief.

The Brain Science of Belief

Beliefs don't just exist in the mind; they live in the brain.

Neuroscience of Belief:

- **The Reticular Activating System (RAS)**: This part of the brain filters reality, showing us information that confirms what we already believe and blocking out contradictions.[5]
- **The Amygdala**: The emotional center of the brain— when a belief is tied to strong emotions, it becomes almost impossible to change.[6]

---

[5] Ray, Amit. "Reticular Activating System for Manifestation and Visualization." *Amit Ray, amitray. com* 1.5 (2021): 3-5.

[6] Kaplan, Jonas T., Sarah I. Gimbel, and Sam Harris. "Neural correlates of maintaining one's political beliefs in the face of counterevidence." *Scientific reports* 6.1 (2016): 39589.

- **The Prefrontal Cortex**: The part of the brain responsible for critical thinking[7]—this is where we challenge or refine beliefs, but only if we are open to change.

Confirmation Bias: The Reason People Don't Change Their Minds

People do not believe what is true. They believe what feels true.

This is why political debates rarely convert the other side. Once a belief is emotionally charged, facts don't matter. If someone believes Trump is a savior, or that he is a threat to democracy, their brain actively filters out any evidence to the contrary.

The same applies to personal beliefs. If you believe you are unworthy of success, your brain will highlight every failure and ignore every success. If you believe you are destined for greatness, you will find evidence to support that, too.

The Power (and Danger) of Unshakable Belief

History has been shaped by people whose beliefs were so strong that they ignored doubt, criticism, or logic.

Belief as a Superpower:

- Steve Jobs believed he could change the world through technology—so he did.
- Elon Musk believes in colonizing Mars—so he builds rockets.

---

[7] Pinto, Anabela A., and Peter Bright. "The biology of resilient beliefs." *Current Ethology* 15.1 (2016): 30-54.

- Oprah Winfrey believed she could rise above poverty—so she did.

Belief as a Weapon:

- Hitler believed in Aryan supremacy—so he led a genocide.
- Jim Jones believed he was a prophet—so he convinced 900 people to drink poison.
- Terrorists believe in a cause so strongly that they are willing to die for it.

Belief is not inherently good or bad—it is simply a tool. The question is: Who is wielding it, and for what purpose?

How to Harness the Power of Belief

If belief can move nations, it can also move you. The secret is learning how to shape your beliefs intentionally rather than letting them be shaped for you.

Step 1: Identify Your Core Beliefs

- What do you believe about yourself? (Are you worthy? Capable? Strong?)
- What do you believe about success? (Is it luck? Hard work? Impossible?)
- What do you believe about your future? (Are you in control, or are you a victim of fate?)

Your current beliefs run your life. If they are not serving you, it's time to change them.

Step 2: Challenge Your Limiting Beliefs

- If you believe you are bad at business, ask: Is that true, or is it just a story I tell myself?

- If you believe success is for other people, ask: What proof do I have that I cannot succeed?
- If you believe you are not enough, ask: Who told me that? And why should I believe them?

Step 3: Reinforce Empowering Beliefs

- Use repetition: Say it, write it, live it. (Daily self-affirming statements work.)
- Attach emotion: Feel it deeply. The brain learns through emotion.
- Find evidence: Every small success reinforces the belief that bigger success is possible.

Belief Is the Ultimate Advantage

Trump, like all powerful leaders, understands something most people do not: belief is reality.

- If you believe you are powerless, you will act powerless.
- If you believe you can change the world, you will find a way to do it.

The world is moved by those who believe in something so deeply that they refuse to be stopped. The questions are:

What do you believe? And how will that belief shape your life?

Chapter 3

Belief in Leadership – The Trump Case Study

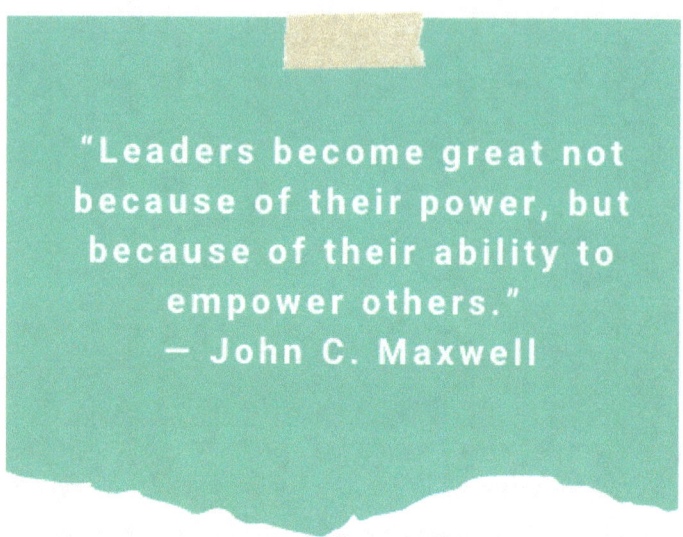

"Leaders become great not because of their power, but because of their ability to empower others."
— John C. Maxwell

The Leader Who Believed His Way to Power

Donald J. Trump's rise from real estate mogul to reality TV star to President of the United States is a masterclass in the power of belief.[8] Regardless of one's political stance, one fact remains: he believed in himself with unshakable certainty—and millions followed.

While his policies, rhetoric, and leadership style remain divisive, the core force behind his success is not wealth or strategy—it is his ability to shape belief. He crafted a movement

---

[8] Pfiffner, James P. "The unusual presidency of Donald Trump." *Political Insight* 8.2 (2017): 9-11.

based not on policy details, but on a simple, emotionally charged belief: *America is broken, and I am the one to fix it.*

The world's most influential leaders—whether admired or feared—do not merely present ideas; they instill belief. Trump's case offers a powerful example of how belief can shape public perception, drive loyalty, and fuel movements.

The Core Beliefs That Built Trump's Leadership

The Unshakable Self-Belief

From the beginning, Trump has projected an image of absolute confidence. He never admits defeat, never acknowledges weakness, and always frames himself as the ultimate winner.

- "I'm a very stable genius."
- "I alone can fix it."
- "Nobody knows [X] better than me."

These statements are not just bravado—they are beliefs. Trump acts as if success is inevitable, and this certainty makes others believe in him, too.

The Power of Simplified, Repeated Beliefs

Trump understands the power of a single, memorable belief. He doesn't overcomplicate his messaging. Instead, he distills complex issues into emotionally charged slogans:

- "Make America Great Again."
- "Build the Wall."
- "America First."

These statements are not detailed policies, but they don't need to be. They create beliefs in the minds of his supporters—beliefs that America has fallen, that outsiders are to blame, and that Trump is the answer.

The 'Us vs. Them' Belief System

Throughout history, leaders who create strong, loyal followings do so by defining a clear enemy.

- Hitler blamed Jews for Germany's decline.[9]
- Revolutionaries blamed monarchs for oppression.
- Religious movements often define 'non-believers' as the enemy.

Trump used this same psychological strategy:

- The Media → "Fake news."
- The Establishment → "The deep state."
- Immigrants → "They're taking our jobs."

By defining "them," he gave his supporters a reason to fight for "us." This created an emotional bond, reinforcing the belief that following him was an act of patriotism.

---

[9] Sletvold, Jon, and Doris Brothers. "The Embodiment of 'Us and Them': Fascist Experience in a Traumatized World." *Ricerca Psicoanalitica* 32.2 (2021): 359-371.

The Science of Why People Follow Leaders Who Believe in Themselves

Certainty Creates Influence

People crave certainty.[10] A leader who believes in themselves without hesitation attracts followers because certainty feels safe.

- The more confidently a belief is expressed, the more people trust it.
- A strong belief overrides facts if delivered with enough conviction.

Trump's absolute self-confidence made his followers feel certain—certain that he would win, certain that he was right, certain that he was their only hope.

Repetition Wires the Brain

Neuroscience shows that repeated exposure to a message strengthens belief. The brain forms neural pathways based on repetition.[11]

Trump repeats messages endlessly:

- "We will win so much you'll get tired of winning."
- "It's a rigged system."

---

[10] Kruglanski, Arie W., and Edward Orehek. "The need for certainty as a psychological nexus for individuals and society." *Extremism and the psychology of uncertainty* (2012): 3-18.

[11] Grill-Spector, Kalanit, Richard Henson, and Alex Martin. "Repetition and the brain: neural models of stimulus-specific effects." *Trends in cognitive sciences* 10.1 (2006): 14-23.

- "The election was stolen."

By hearing the same phrases over and over, supporters' brains reinforce these ideas as truth, making them harder to challenge.

Emotion Over Logic

People don't follow leaders because of logic; they follow because of emotion.[12] Trump's speeches are filled with anger, pride, fear, and hope. This emotional intensity makes his beliefs contagious.

- Fear of immigrants → "They're bringing drugs, they're bringing crime."
- Hope for revival → "We're going to bring back jobs."
- Pride in identity → "America first!"

These emotions anchor beliefs deeply into the unconscious mind, making them resistant to change.

Belief in Leadership: Lessons for Anyone

Trump's rise is not an anomaly. His success follows the universal laws of belief-based leadership. Whether in politics, business, or social movements, the same principles apply:

Speak with Absolute Certainty

If you want people to believe in you, believe in yourself first.

- Say it like it's already true. ("I am successful." "I will make this happen.")

---

[12] Michie, Susan, and Janaki Gooty. "Values, emotions, and authenticity: Will the real leader please stand up?." *The Leadership Quarterly* 16.3 (2005): 441-457.

- Remove doubt from your language. ("I might" → "I will.")
- Show confidence, even in failure. (Trump never acknowledges loss—he reframes it.)

Keep It Simple and Repeat It

- Find one clear message that defines your purpose.
- Say it again and again until it becomes truth to those who hear it.
- People don't follow complexity—they follow clarity.

Create an 'Us vs. Them' Narrative (Ethically)

This does not mean creating division, but defining a mission.

- MLK: "We will not be judged by the color of our skin." (Us = justice, Them = oppression.)
- Elon Musk: "We must colonize Mars to save humanity." (Us = visionaries, Them = doubters.)
- **Your own mission:** Define what you stand for and what you stand against.

The Double-Edged Sword of Belief-Based Leadership

Trump's case teaches us something critical: belief is a tool, not inherently good or bad.

The Double-Edged Sword of Belief-Based Leadership

A belief in freedom can liberate millions.

A belief in superiority can destroy nations.

A belief in yourself can change your life.

The question is, how you will use belief?

This book is not about politics. It is about understanding the raw, undeniable power of belief—and learning to wield it consciously.

The leaders who shape history are not necessarily the smartest or the richest. They are the ones who believe, without doubt, in their own vision.

Chapter 4

The Trump Playbook – A Breakdown of His Books

"If you're going to be thinking, you may as well think big." — Donald J. Trump

How Trump's Books Showcase the Power of Belief

Donald Trump has written or co-authored several books, each reinforcing a core belief system that shaped his brand, business, and political career. Whether one agrees with him or not, his books serve as a blueprint for understanding how belief, when consistently applied, can shape reality.

In this chapter, we'll dissect Trump's major books to uncover how he uses belief—both for himself and to influence others.

Trump: The Art of the Deal (1987): The Power of Big Thinking

Key Belief: "Think big, act bold, and never settle for less."

Trump's first and most famous book, *Trump: The Art of the Deal*[13], outlines his philosophy on negotiation and success. His core belief? Success is about confidence and controlling the narrative.

Main Takeaways:

- **Reality is negotiable**: Trump argues that business deals aren't just about numbers but about shaping perception. If you believe you deserve more, others will, too.
- **Thinking small is a failure mindset**: He urges readers to remove limitations and think on a massive scale.

---

[13] Trump, Donald J., Donald Trump, and Tony Schwartz. *Trump: The art of the deal*. Random House Digital, Inc., 2005.

- **Control the story**: Whether in business or media, he who controls the narrative wins.

How It Connects to Belief:

- This book shows how belief in oneself transforms how others see you.
- Confidence in negotiations often determines the outcome more than logic.
- It teaches that repetition creates truth—if you say you're the best long enough, people start to believe it.

Trump: The Art of Survival (1991): Belief in Resilience

Key Belief: "No matter how hard you fall, you can rise again."

This book came after Trump's financial struggles in the early 1990s, when his businesses faced bankruptcy.[14] Instead of admitting defeat, Trump reframed his failure as a learning experience and positioned himself as a comeback story.

Main Takeaways:

- Failure is temporary if you believe in your ability to rebound.
- Never admit weakness publicly. Trump emphasizes that even in the worst moments, projecting strength keeps opportunities alive.
- Confidence creates second chances. His ability to maintain a strong public image allowed him to recover financially.

---

[14] *The Art of Survival*: Trump, Donald J., and Charles Leerhsen. *The Art of Survival*. Warner Books, 1991.

How It Connects to Belief:

- This book demonstrates the power of reframing reality.
- Trump's belief in himself allowed him to recover when others would have quit.
- It teaches that your mindset dictates your comeback.

The America We Deserve (2000): Vision as Belief

Key Belief: "A great leader must sell a compelling vision of the future."

In *The America We Deserve*[15], Trump foreshadows his future presidential run by outlining his political beliefs. The book is less about policies and more about his vision for America.

Main Takeaways:

- A strong belief system attracts followers. Trump repeatedly emphasizes a clear vision: America can be great again.
- Create urgency. He argues that the country is in decline and needs strong leadership to fix it—this instills a sense of crisis, making people more receptive to belief-based leadership.
- Tap into emotion. Trump focuses on patriotism, pride, and frustration, using emotional triggers to make his ideas resonate.

How It Connects to Belief:

- People follow leaders who believe in their vision with conviction.

---

[15] Trump, Donald. *The America we deserve*. Renaissance Books, 2000.

- Repetition of a simple idea (America's decline and revival) shapes public perception.
- Emotional appeals override rational arguments—belief spreads faster through feelings than facts.

Think Like a Billionaire (2005): Mindset Over Circumstance

Key Belief: "Wealth starts in the mind, not the bank account."

This book serves as a mindset manual for success. Trump argues that people who think like billionaires attract wealth and opportunities.[16]

Main Takeaways:

- Self-perception shapes reality. If you see yourself as successful, others will too.
- Rich people think differently. They focus on opportunity, not obstacles.
- Act like you belong. Trump believes that confidence and presentation create influence.

How It Connects to Belief:

- This book reinforces the idea that belief in oneself creates external success.
- It demonstrates how mindset determines financial and social opportunities.

---

[16] Trump, Donald J., and Meredith McIver. *Trump: Think like a billionaire: Everything you need to know about success, real estate, and life.* Ballantine Books, 2005.

- Thinking big leads to acting big, which leads to bigger results.

Great Again: How to fix our crippled America (2016)[17]: Belief as a Political Weapon

Key Belief: "America is broken, and I am the only one who can fix it."

This book became the foundation of Trump's presidential campaign. It focused less on policies and more on belief systems that mobilize people.

Main Takeaways:

- Create a sense of urgency. Trump paints a bleak picture of America's decline, making people feel a need for immediate change.
- Position yourself as the savior. He presents himself as the only person strong enough to restore greatness.
- Use repetition to reinforce belief. Simple phrases like "Make America Great Again" became ingrained in public consciousness.

How It Connects to Belief:

- It shows how belief, not policy, wins elections.
- Emotional conviction moves people more than facts.
- It demonstrates the power of a unifying message.

---

[17] Trump, Donald. *Great again: How to fix our crippled America.* Simon and Schuster, 2016.

The Trump Playbook: The Three Pillars of Belief-Based Success

Across all of Trump's books, three core principles emerge:

1. Self-Belief is the Foundation of Influence

- If you don't believe in yourself, no one else will.
- Confidence creates opportunities.
- Never waver in projecting certainty.

2. Perception is More Important Than Reality

- People don't follow truth; they follow what they believe is true.
- Control the narrative—whoever tells the best story wins.
- Speak boldly and consistently to shape public perception.

3. Emotions Drive Belief More Than Facts

- People believe what they feel more than what they analyze.
- A compelling vision and clear enemy (e.g., "the establishment") create strong loyalty.
- Repetition and simplicity strengthen belief.

How to Use These Lessons in Your Own Life

1. Apply Unshakable Self-Belief

- Adopt a "winner's mindset" in everything you do.
- Speak with confidence, even before results show up.
- Never let failure define your identity—reframe it as learning.

2. Control Your Narrative

- Define what you want to be known for and repeat it relentlessly.
- Craft a clear, powerful message about your mission.
- Make others see you as you want to be seen.

3. Use Emotion to Strengthen Belief

- People follow passion, not facts—so lead with energy.
- Create a sense of urgency around your goals.
- Make your message simple, repeatable, and memorable.

Final Thoughts: Belief is a Tool—How Will You Use It?

Trump's books reveal a truth larger than politics: belief moves the world.

- It can build empires or destroy them.
- It can create movements of hope or fear.
- It can elevate or manipulate.

The question is: How will YOU wield belief?

PART II

Building Your Personal Belief System

Chapter 5

How to Build an Unshakable Belief System for Yourself

"Whether you think you can or you think you can't, you're right."
— Henry Ford

Belief is the foundation of every major success, revolution, and transformation in history. It has built nations, fueled social movements, and created billionaires. But it has also been used to manipulate, deceive, and destroy.

The question is: How do YOU harness the power of belief to shape your life, influence others, and leave a lasting impact on the world?

This chapter will give you a step-by-step system to build an unshakable belief system—one that empowers you to achieve your goals, influence your environment, and create a legacy.

The Science of Belief: How It Shapes Reality

Beliefs are not just abstract thoughts; they reprogram your brain.

1. Your Brain Reinforces What You Believe

- The Reticular Activating System (RAS)[18] filters information, prioritizing what aligns with your beliefs.
- If you believe you're lucky, your brain actively notices opportunities.
- If you believe you're a failure, your brain highlights mistakes and setbacks.

---

[18] Arguinchona, Joseph H., and Prasanna Tadi. "Neuroanatomy, reticular activating system." (2019).

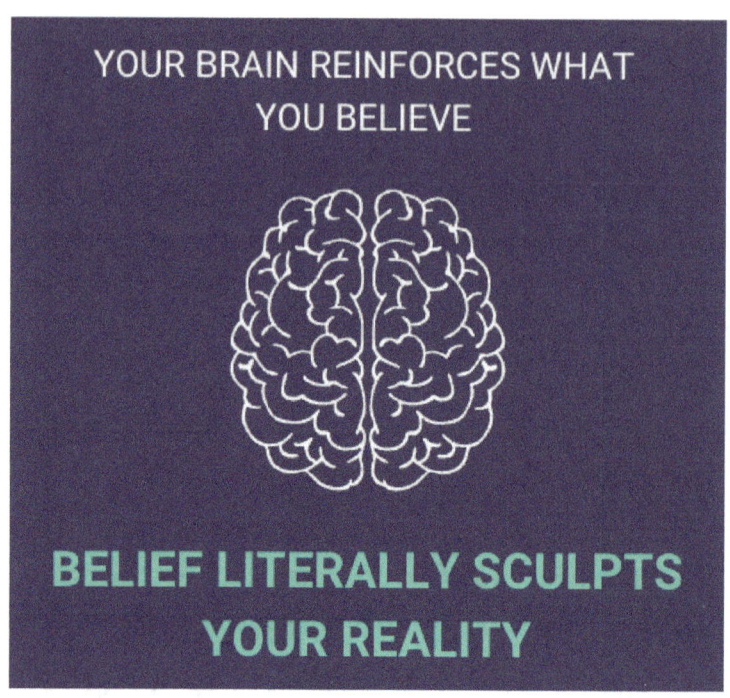

YOUR BRAIN REINFORCES WHAT YOU BELIEVE

BELIEF LITERALLY SCULPTS YOUR REALITY

2. Belief Influences Your Body

- Studies show that placebo effects (fake treatments) can produce real healing—because the patient believes they are getting better.[19]
- Athletes who visualize themselves winning enhance their actual performance.
- Belief changes your hormones, body language, and energy.

---

[19] Ray, Oakley. "How the mind hurts and heals the body." *American psychologist* 59.1 (2004): 29.

3. Belief is Contagious

- Charismatic leaders influence others because they believe in their vision so deeply.[20]
- People unconsciously mirror the energy and conviction of those around them.
- The strongest belief in a room dominates.

Step 1: Define Your Core Belief System

Before you can create unshakable belief, you need clarity.

Ask Yourself These Questions:

1. What do I believe about success?
2. What do I believe about failure?
3. What do I believe about myself?
4. What do I believe is possible in my lifetime?

Exercise: Write your answers down. If your beliefs are limiting (e.g., "I'm not lucky," "Success is for other people"), please rewrite them.

New belief system:

- Old belief: "I always struggle financially."
- New belief: "I create wealth by spotting and seizing opportunities."

Your brain will fight you at first. But repetition rewires your unconscious mind.

---

[20] Conger, Jay A., Rabindra N. Kanungo, and Sanjay T. Menon. "Charismatic leadership and follower effects." *Journal of Organizational Behavior: The International Journal of Industrial, Occupational and Organizational Psychology and Behavior* 21.7 (2000): 747-767.

Step 2: Rewire Your Mind for Unbreakable Confidence

Confidence isn't something you're born with—it's something you train.

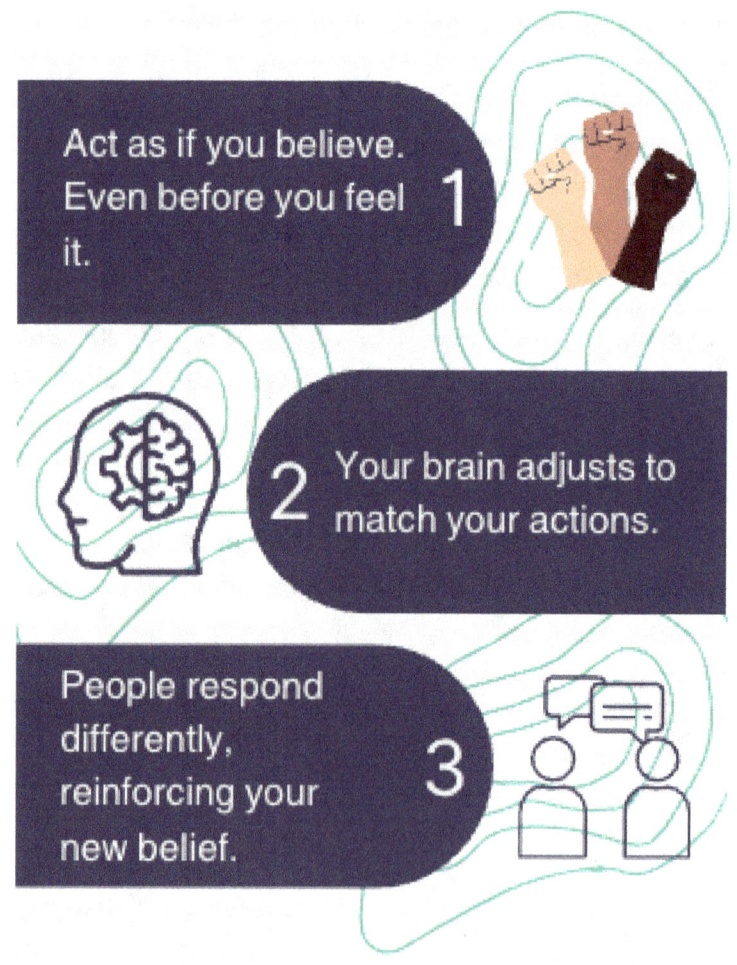

The Confidence Loop

1. Act as if you believe. Even before you feel it.

2. Your brain adjusts to match your actions.

3. People respond differently, reinforcing your new belief.

Tools to Strengthen Your Belief:

✓ **Self-Affirming Statements** – Speak new beliefs out loud daily.

✓ **Visualization** – Picture yourself achieving your biggest goal every morning.

✓ **Micro-wins** – Start with small successes to build momentum.

Step 3: Master the Art of Conviction

The world follows those who believe in something with unshakable conviction.

How to Speak & Act with Conviction:

- Speak in absolutes, not hesitations. Say, "I will," not "I'll try."
- Repeat your beliefs until they become reality. (Trump's Make America Great Again is a masterclass in this.)
- Use bold, decisive language. People don't follow those who doubt themselves.

✓ Wrong: "I hope this works out."

✓ Right: "I know I will make this happen."

Step 4: Train Your Mind to See Opportunities, Not Obstacles

Belief systems determine whether you see doors or dead ends.

✓ Fixed mindset: "That's impossible."

✓ Growth mindset: "There's always a way."

How to Reprogram Your Perception:

✓ Ask empowering questions. Instead of "Why does this always happen to me?" ask, "How can I use this to my advantage?"

✓ Reframe failures as lessons. Every loss contains a hidden advantage—find it.

✓ Surround yourself with believers. Your environment reinforces your mindset.

Step 5: Use Belief to Influence and Lead

The greatest leaders in history were masters of belief.

How to Influence Others Through Your Belief System:

✓ Speak with certainty. People follow confidence, not hesitation.

✓ Tell powerful stories. Facts inform, but stories persuade.

✓ Repeat your message relentlessly. Repetition solidifies belief.

✓ Use emotion, not just logic. Logic makes people think; emotion makes them act.

Example: Why did Make America Great Again work?

- It was simple, emotional, and repeated endlessly.
- It created a clear vision and an enemy (the establishment).
- It tapped into deep desires and frustrations.

Use the same formula for your own mission.

Step 6: Cement Your Legacy – Use Your Belief to Change the World

The final step is taking massive action.

✓ Define your mission. What impact will you leave behind?

✓ Speak it into existence. The world must hear it over and over.

✓ Take fearless action. Confidence grows in motion, not in thought.

✓ Turn your belief into a movement. When others believe, your influence multiplies.

Final Thought: The World is Moved by Those Who Believe

Belief is a tool. It can build, or it can destroy. It can elevate or manipulate.

The question is: How will YOU use it?

This book isn't just about Trump. It's about YOU.

- You can shape reality.
- You can transform your life.
- You can lead others to something greater.

But first, you must believe it.

Chapter 6

The Psychology of Mass Movements – How Beliefs Shape History

"All great movements are popular movements. They are the volcanic eruptions of human passions and emotions." — Adolf Hitler, Mein Kampf

"The only thing we have to fear is fear itself." — Franklin D. Roosevelt

Belief is the most powerful force in history. It can build civilizations, start revolutions, and launch industries. It can also destroy nations, justify atrocities, and enslave minds.

But what makes a belief so powerful that it moves millions? Why do people follow one leader but reject another? And most importantly—how can you use this knowledge to create a belief system that inspires, empowers, and transforms?

This chapter will dissect how mass movements form, thrive, and sometimes collapse—so you can learn to harness belief for yourself.

Step 1: Every Mass Movement Starts with a Simple, Emotional Idea

At the core of every movement is one powerful belief that resonates deeply.

✓ Religious movements: "God has chosen us."

✓ Political revolutions: "The system is corrupt. We must overthrow it."

✓ Social movements: "We are being oppressed. Justice must be served."

✓ Business empires: "We are building the future."

The Best Beliefs Are

• • •

✔ **Simple** – Easy to remember and repeat

✔ **Emotional** – They tap into fear, hope, or anger

✔ **Universal** – They make people feel part of something bigger

Example:

- "Make America Great Again" – Simple, emotional, nostalgic
- "Yes We Can" (Obama) – Inclusive, hopeful, empowering
- "Workers of the world, unite!" (Marxism) – Direct, urgent, collective

Your Takeaway:

If you want to create a powerful belief system, simplify your message and make it emotional.

Step 2: The Role of an Enemy – Why Movements Need Opposition

Every great movement creates an enemy to fight against.

✓ Religions have the Devil.

✓ Revolutions have corrupt governments.

✓ Social movements have oppressors.

✓ Companies have competitors.

Example:

- Trump vs. "The Deep State" – A vague but powerful enemy
- Apple vs. Microsoft – "We're the rebels, they're the boring corporate machine"
- Christianity vs. Satan – The ultimate battle of good vs. evil

Why does this work?

- The brain craves contrast[21]. We understand the world in opposites (light vs. dark, us vs. them).
- Conflict fuels passion. If there's a struggle, people feel invested.
- Enemies unite people. Nothing bonds a group like a shared enemy.

---

[21] Clark, Eve V. "On the logic of contrast." *Journal of Child language* 15.2 (1988): 317-335.

Your Takeaway:

If you want to build a movement, define what you are against just as clearly as what you stand for.

Step 3: The Power of Repetition – How Ideas Become Reality

The human brain believes what it hears repeatedly.[22]

✓ Religious mantras are repeated daily.

✓ Hitler's propaganda was drilled into people's minds.

✓ Advertising slogans are repeated until they become second nature.

Example:

- Trump repeated "Fake News" until it became widely accepted.[23]
- Nike's "Just Do It" has been ingrained in our culture.
- Revolutions chant the same slogans over and over.

Your Takeaway:

If you want people to believe in something, say it over and over.

---

[22] Fazio, Lisa K., Nadia M. Brashier, B. Keith Payne, and Elizabeth J. Marsh. "Knowledge Does Not Protect Against Illusory Truth." *Journal of Experimental Psychology: General*, vol. 144, no. 5, 2015, pp. 993–1002. https://doi.org/10.1037/xge0000098.

[23] Bowman, Nicholas David, and Elizabeth Cohen. "Mental shortcuts, emotion, and social rewards: the challenges of detecting and resisting fake news." *Fake news: Understanding media and misinformation in the digital age* (2020): 235-243.

Step 4: The Leader Effect – How Charisma Fuels Movements

Movements don't just need ideas; they need a face.

✓ Jesus, Muhammad, and Buddha – Religious figures who embodied their teachings

✓ Hitler, Stalin, Mao – Political leaders who became symbols

✓ Elon Musk, Steve Jobs – Business leaders who made people believe in their vision

What makes a leader effective?

✓ Absolute conviction – People follow those who believe in themselves.

✓ A clear mission – No one follows confusion.

✓ Unshakable confidence – Indecision kills belief.

Example:

- Trump speaks with absolute confidence, even when facts are against him.
- Martin Luther King Jr. inspired millions with a clear, emotional mission.
- Elon Musk convinces investors by acting like the future is already happening.

Your Takeaway:

If you want to influence others, speak with conviction and embody your beliefs.

Step 5: Turning Belief into Action – How Movements Change the World

A belief is useless unless it leads to action.

✓ Religions demand rituals. (Prayer, fasting, ceremonies)

✓ Revolutions demand protests.

✓ Companies demand customer loyalty.

Example:

- The Civil Rights Movement used sit-ins and marches to force change.
- Trump rallies kept supporters engaged and energized.
- Tesla turned customers into brand evangelists.

Your Takeaway:

If you want a belief to last, it must lead to real-world action.

The Dark Side: When Belief Becomes Dangerous

Belief can be used for good—or to control and manipulate.

✓ Cult leaders use belief to isolate followers.

✓ Dictators use belief to justify violence.

✓ Scammers use belief to steal money.

Example:

- Nazi Germany – A powerful belief system weaponized for destruction
- Jonestown Massacre – A charismatic leader convinced 900+ people to commit suicide

- Crypto scams – People are told to "HODL[24]" even as they lose everything

Your Takeaway:

Always question: Who benefits from this belief?

Conclusion: The Choice is Yours

Belief has built empires and destroyed civilizations. It has created the greatest works of art and justified the worst atrocities.

But now you understand how it works.

YOU ☰
CAN ↘

☐ **Use belief to change your life.**

☐ **You can use belief to influence others.**

☐ **You can use belief to leave a lasting legacy.**

But how you use it—for good or bad—is up to you.

---

[24] Hold On for Dear Life

Next Steps: The Book That Will Change Everything

This book isn't just an analysis—it's a blueprint for action.

Coming up in Chapter 7: How to Take These Principles and Apply Them to Your Own Life.

> ✓ Want to build a movement? This will show you how.

> ✓ Want to create unshakable confidence? The steps are here.

> ✓ Want to leave a lasting impact? This is your guide.

Are you ready for Chapter 7: The Blueprint for Personal Mastery?

Chapter 7

The Blueprint for Personal Mastery – How to Use the Power of Belief to Transform Your Life

Belief is the single most powerful force in human psychology.[25] It can shape your destiny, dictate your success, and determine whether you live a life of greatness or mediocrity.

Now that we've analyzed how belief moves history, it's time to bring that power into your own life.

In this chapter, we will create a step-by-step system for harnessing belief to:

✓ Master your mind and eliminate self-doubt

✓ Develop unshakable confidence in your vision

✓ Inspire others and build a movement around your ideas

✓ Achieve extraordinary results in any area of life

Let's begin.

Step 1: Choose a Belief That Empowers You

What do you believe about yourself? About success? About what's possible?

Most people never examine their beliefs. They inherit them—from parents, society, or past failures. But if you want to master belief, you must choose what to believe.

✓ Fixed vs. Growth Mindset

- Fixed Mindset: "I'm not good at this." → Leads to stagnation.

---

[25] Lipton, Bruce H. *The Biology of Belief: Unleashing the Power of Consciousness, Matter & Miracles*. 10th Anniversary ed., Hay House, Inc., 2015.

- Growth Mindset: "I can get better at anything." → Leads to mastery.

✓ Scarcity vs. Abundance Belief

- Scarcity: "Success is limited. If others win, I lose."
- Abundance: "There's more than enough for everyone."

✓ Victim vs. Ownership Mentality

- Victim: "Life happens to me."
- Ownership: "I create my reality."

✓ Example:

- Steve Jobs believed: "People don't know what they want until you show them."
- Oprah Winfrey believed: "I create my own destiny."
- Elon Musk believed: "The future belongs to those who build it."

Your Takeaway:

Pick a belief that serves you. If you don't choose your beliefs, someone else will.

Step 2: Reprogram Your Mind Through Repetition

Your brain accepts what it hears repeatedly.

✓ Religions use mantras and prayers to ingrain beliefs.

✓ Political movements use slogans to shape thought.

✓ Athletes use affirmations to build confidence.

If you want to master belief, you must program your own mind.

✓ Daily Self-Affirmation Rituals:

- Write down one belief you want to install.
- Say it out loud every morning and night.
- Visualize yourself living that belief.
- Repeat this for 30 days.

✓ Example:

- "I am a leader who inspires millions."
- "I create my own success."
- "I am unstoppable."

Your Takeaway:

Repetition is the secret weapon of belief. Use it.

Step 3: Build an Environment That Reinforces Your Belief

Your belief is only as strong as the environment that supports it.

✓ If you surround yourself with negative people, you will doubt yourself.

✓ If you consume weak ideas, you will have weak beliefs.

✓ If you live in an environment that reinforces success, you will grow.

✓ Action Plan:

1. Audit your social circle.
   - Remove people who make you doubt yourself.
   - Add people who inspire you.

2. Control your inputs.
   - Read books that fuel your belief.
   - Follow mentors and thought leaders who embody it.

3. Create a physical environment that aligns with your belief.
   - Want to be a leader? Surround yourself with leadership books and mentors.
   - Want to be an entrepreneur? Work in spaces that inspire innovation.

✓ *Example:*

- Steve Jobs designed his home to stimulate creativity.
- Elon Musk surrounds himself with people who think on a massive scale.
- Successful athletes train in environments that push them beyond their limits.

Your Takeaway:

Your environment is stronger than willpower. Shape it wisely.

Step 4: Take Bold Action That Strengthens Your Belief

Belief is not just mental. It is reinforced by action.

✓ If you act with courage, you become courageous.

✓ If you act with confidence, you become confident.

✓ If you act like a leader, you become a leader.

The Power of Bold Moves

- Muhammad Ali called himself "The Greatest" before the world believed it.
- Elon Musk bet his entire fortune on Tesla and SpaceX.
- Oprah Winfrey acted like a media mogul before she became one.

Action Plan:

- Identify one action that aligns with your belief.
- Do it immediately.
- Repeat until belief becomes identity.

✓ *Example:*

- Want to believe you are a leader? Start leading today.
- Want to believe you are fearless? Do something that scares you.
- Want to believe you are successful? Start behaving like it now.

Your Takeaway:

Your beliefs are shaped by your actions. Act first. Believe second.

Step 5: Teach Others to Reinforce Your Belief

The fastest way to solidify a belief is to teach it to others.

✓ If you share an idea, you own it.

✓ If you inspire others, your belief strengthens.

✓ If you become a leader, your belief becomes unshakable.

✓ Example:

- Tony Robbins teaches confidence—so he becomes more confident.
- Elon Musk shares his vision—so it becomes more real.
- Martin Luther King Jr. repeated his dream—so the world started believing it.

✓ Action Plan:

- Teach your belief to at least one person today.
- Share your vision on social media, in conversations, or in writing.
- The more you teach, the stronger your belief becomes.

Your Takeaway:

Teaching is the final step of mastery. Share your belief and it will grow.

The Ultimate Test: Can You Prove Your Belief in the Real World?

Belief is nothing without proof.

If you truly believe something, your life should reflect it.

✓ Want to be a leader? You should be leading.

✓ Want to be successful? Your habits should reflect success.

✓ Want to change the world? You should already be making an impact.

✓ *The Final Challenge:*

- What do you believe about yourself?
- Does your life reflect that belief?
- If not, what will you do TODAY to prove it?

Conclusion: This is Your Moment

Now you know the blueprint.

✓ You understand how belief shapes history.

✓ You know how to program your own mind.

✓ You have a step-by-step system to take control of your belief.

The only question is: Will you use it?

This book isn't just about knowledge. It's about action.

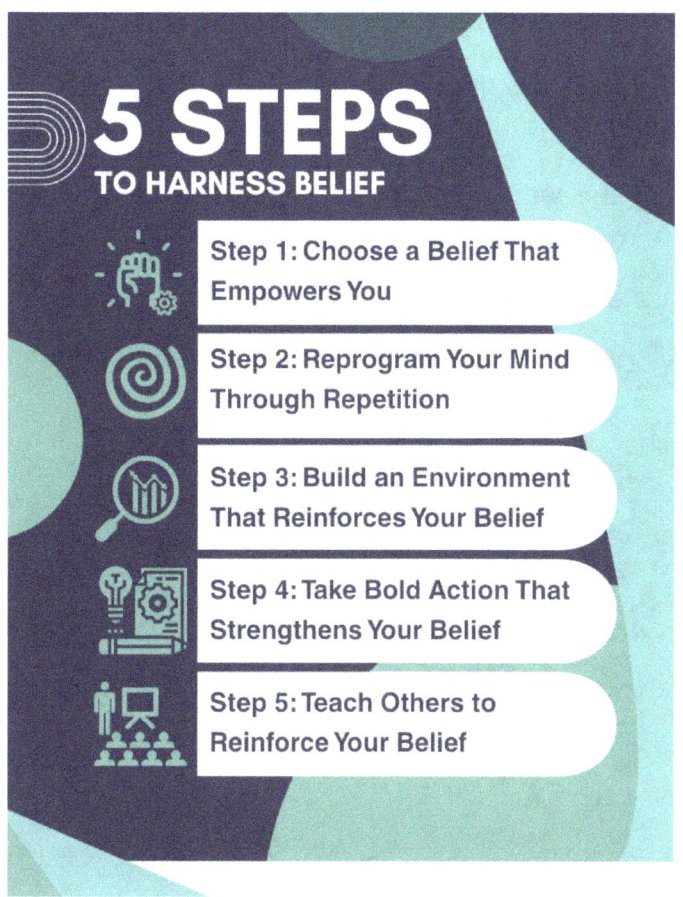

5 STEPS

TO HARNESS BELIEF

Step 1: Choose a Belief That Empowers You

Step 2: Reprogram Your Mind Through Repetition

Step 3: Build an Environment That Reinforces Your Belief

Step 4: Take Bold Action That Strengthens Your Belief

Step 5: Teach Others to Reinforce Your Belief

Your Next Step:

✓ Pick one belief that will change your life.

✓ Reinforce it through repetition.

✓ Take bold action to prove it.

✓ Shape your environment to support it.

✓ Teach it to others to make it unshakable.

If you do this, your life will never be the same.

Next: Chapter 8 – The Belief Systems of the World's Greatest Leaders

Are you ready to unlock the secret beliefs that built empires, inspired revolutions, and shaped the world?

Let's continue. History is waiting.

Chapter 8

The Belief Systems of the World's Greatest Leaders

The leaders who have changed the world are not necessarily the smartest, the most skilled, or the most talented. What sets them apart is their unwavering belief in something bigger than themselves. Their belief systems are the fuel that drives their extraordinary actions, and it is this belief that we must study if we are to understand how to move the world.

In this chapter, we will analyze the belief systems of the world's greatest leaders, from Mahatma Gandhi to Nelson Mandela, and from Winston Churchill to Margaret Thatcher. By studying their mindsets, we will uncover the principles that powered their success and how you can apply these to your own journey.

The Belief Systems of Great Leaders: What Makes Them Unstoppable?

1. Mahatma Gandhi: Nonviolent Resistance and the Power of Peace

Core Belief: "You must be the change you wish to see in the world."

Gandhi's belief in nonviolent resistance was revolutionary. In a world dominated by war and colonial oppression, Gandhi's unwavering belief in the power of peace and truth inspired millions to rise up without resorting to violence.[26]

---

[26] Gandhi, M. K. "My Faith in Non-violence." *Mahatma Gandhi's Views on Peace, Nonviolence and Conflict Resolution,* www.mkgandhi.org/nonviolence/faithin_nonvio.php.

What We Can Learn:

- **Nonviolence**: Gandhi's belief that "an eye for an eye makes the whole world blind" teaches us that our actions must reflect our values. Belief in peace, non-violence, and reconciliation can change the course of history.
- **Resilience**: Gandhi believed that the best way to fight injustice was not through anger but through peaceful action and personal sacrifice.
- **Application**: Choose compassion over confrontation and resolve conflicts with integrity. Use your belief in peace as a tool for social change.

Actionable Tip: Cultivate inner peace by meditating daily, practicing patience, and finding non-violent ways to resolve conflicts.

2. Nelson Mandela: Forgiveness and the Power of Unity

Core Belief: "I have walked that long road to freedom. I have tried not to falter; I have made missteps along the way. But I have discovered the secret that after climbing a great hill, one only finds that there are many more hills to climb."

Mandela's belief in the power of forgiveness and unity shaped the destiny of South Africa. He spent 27 years in prison, yet he emerged with a belief that no matter the past, it was unity and reconciliation that would transform his country.[27]

---

[27] Mandela, Nelson. "Address by President Nelson Mandela to the Interfaith Commissioning Service for the Truth and Reconciliation Commission." *South African History Online*, 13 Feb. 1996,

What We Can Learn:

- **Forgiveness as Freedom**: Mandela understood that holding onto resentment only shackles you. His belief in forgiving his enemies created a new sense of possibility for South Africa.
- **Unity for Greater Purpose**: He believed that, despite the deep wounds of apartheid, only through unity could his country achieve peace.
- **Application**: If Mandela could forgive those who oppressed him, we can all choose to forgive and seek common ground with those who oppose us.

Actionable Tip: Find a situation in your life where you are holding onto resentment, and practice the art of forgiveness. It is only by healing wounds that you create the space for true unity.

3. Winston Churchill: Resilience and Unyielding Determination

Core Belief: "Never, never, never give up."

Churchill's belief in the indomitable spirit of the British people during World War II was the cornerstone of his leadership. During the darkest days of the war, when defeat

---

https://sahistory.org.za/archive/address-president-nelson-mandela-interfaith-commissioning-service-truth-and-reconciliation.

seemed inevitable, his belief in victory propelled an entire nation to fight on.[28]

What We Can Learn:

- **Unyielding Belief**: Churchill's mantra was "never give up," a belief that embodies the importance of resilience in the face of adversity. When you are committed to a goal, nothing can stop you.
- **Visionary Leadership**: Churchill believed that his country could overcome any challenge. It was not just about winning the war—it was about protecting values that were essential to the future.
- **Application**: When faced with challenges, remember that perseverance and a clear sense of purpose will guide you through. The world needs leaders who refuse to quit.

Actionable Tip: When challenges arise, write down your core belief and reaffirm your commitment to the cause. Refuse to give up no matter what.

4. Margaret Thatcher: Conviction and the Power of Self-Belief

Core Belief: "Being powerful is like being a lady. If you have to tell people you are, you aren't."

---

[28] Churchill, Winston S. "Blood, Toil, Tears and Sweat." *House of Commons*, 13 May 1940. *International Churchill Society.*

Margaret Thatcher's belief in self-confidence and conviction made her one of the most powerful political figures of the 20th century.[29] She was known for her unyielding stance on issues, and her ability to stand firm in her beliefs, even when faced with extreme opposition.

What We Can Learn:

- **Self-Belief**: Thatcher's success came from an unshakable belief in her principles and abilities. To lead others, you must first believe in yourself.
- **Conviction in Action**: Thatcher's belief was not just about words; it was about consistent actions that aligned with her values. Her success was not due to popularity, but due to staying true to what she believed was right for her country.
- **Application**: When you have a strong belief, don't shy away from standing firm. Lead with confidence and let your actions prove your convictions.

Actionable Tip: Create a list of your core beliefs. Each day, take actions that align with those beliefs, no matter the external pressure.

5. Martin Luther King Jr.: The Dream of a Better Future

Core Belief: "I have a dream that one day little black boys and girls will be holding hands with little white boys and girls."

---

[29] Thatcher, Margaret. *The Downing Street Years*. HarperCollins, 1993.

Martin Luther King Jr. is often remembered for his visionary belief in racial equality and his steadfast commitment to achieving a world of justice. His belief in a better future was the catalyst for one of the most significant social movements in history.[30]

What We Can Learn:

- **Visionary Leadership**: King's ability to articulate a vision of hope motivated millions to believe that change was possible.
- **Belief in Equality**: He believed that all people, regardless of race or background, were entitled to dignity and equality.
- **Application**: Develop a vision that is bigger than yourself—something that can inspire others to believe in a shared future.

Actionable Tip: Take a moment to reflect on your vision for the future. Write it down, and take steps every day to make it a reality.

The Common Thread: Belief and Its Power to Move the World

Across all of these great leaders, there is a common thread that binds them together: *Unshakable belief.* Whether it was Gandhi's belief in nonviolence, Mandela's belief in unity, Churchill's belief in resilience, Thatcher's belief in self-

---

[30] King, Martin Luther, Jr. *I Have a Dream*. Edited by James M. Washington, HarperOne, 1991.

confidence, or King's belief in equality, these leaders all moved the world because they acted on their beliefs.

The Three Pillars of Powerful Belief Systems:

1. **Purpose**: A belief system is driven by a higher purpose that connects to something bigger than the self.
2. **Consistency**: Powerful leaders believe in their ideas with consistency, no matter how difficult the path.
3. **Action**: Belief without action is powerless. Great leaders bring their beliefs to life through consistent action.

3 The Three Pillars of Powerful Belief Systems:

Your Challenge: Become a Leader of Belief

Now that you've studied the belief systems of the world's greatest leaders, it's time for you to apply these lessons. What do you believe in? What is your vision? And how will you act on that belief to inspire others?

Your Takeaway:

The world needs people who believe in something powerful. Become that person.

Next: Chapter 9 – Mastering the Art of Influence: How to Lead and Inspire Others with Your Belief

Ready to take your belief to the next level? In the next chapter, we will dive deep into how to influence others and build a movement around your beliefs. Stay tuned.

PART III

Belief in Action – Influence, Leadership, and Impact

Chapter 9

Mastering the Art of Influence: How to Lead and Inspire Others with Your Belief

The most powerful people in history have not only believed in something deeply, but they have also inspired others to share and follow those beliefs. To lead is to influence—to help others see the world as you see it and to guide them towards a shared vision. But how do you master the art of influence and use your belief to lead with purpose and power?

In this chapter, we'll explore the essential principles of influence, how to inspire others, and how to build a movement around your belief. This isn't just about leadership in a traditional sense—it's about becoming the kind of person who ignites change and moves the world forward.

The Foundations of Influence

1. The Power of a Clear and Compelling Vision

Great leaders are visionary. They see a future that others can't yet see. Their vision isn't just about goals—it's about a belief system that paints a picture of what could be. The more clear and compelling your vision, the more people will be drawn to it.

Example: Steve Jobs built Apple on the belief that technology could change the world and empower people to be creative. Further, Bill Gates's vision of a personal computer for every household was bold, ambitious, and transformative.

What We Can Learn:

- **Clarity is Power**: The more clearly you can articulate your vision, the more people will see the possibility of that future.
- **Inspiration Through Belief**: When your belief is aligned with your vision, it inspires others to follow and believe in that same future.

Actionable Tip: Write down your vision in one sentence. Make it bold and inspirational and use it as a guiding statement in everything you do. Each action you take should be aimed at making this vision a reality.

2. Building Trust: The Foundation of Influence

Trust is the bedrock of any leadership influence. If people don't trust you, they won't follow you, no matter how powerful your vision or how compelling your belief. Trust is built on authenticity, integrity, and consistency.

Example: Oprah Winfrey became one of the most influential figures in the world not just because of her talents, but because she consistently showed up as authentic and vulnerable. People trust her because she has always been genuine, and her belief in others has inspired countless individuals.

What We Can Learn:

- **Authenticity is Key**: Influence begins with being true to yourself. People can sense when you are being authentic, and this builds trust.
- **Consistency Builds Credibility**: Trust is earned through consistent actions that align with your words. If you say you believe in something, prove it with your actions.

Actionable Tip: Take one area of your life where you can be more authentic and consistent. Lead with integrity, and watch how others respond to your authenticity.

3. The Power of Empathy and Connection

Great leaders understand that true influence comes from a place of deep empathy. They know how to connect with others on a human level. When you can make others feel heard, valued, and understood, you unlock the power to influence.

Example: Mother Teresa became a global symbol of compassion not because of her achievements, but because of her empathy and her ability to connect with people in their moments of suffering.[31] Her belief in the inherent dignity of every human being propelled her to do the most selfless work imaginable.

What We Can Learn:

- **Empathy Drives Connection**: To inspire and influence others, you must first understand their needs and connect emotionally with their journey.
- **Leading with Heart**: Influence doesn't come from logic alone; it comes from your ability to understand and respond to others' feelings and needs.

Actionable Tip: In your next conversation or interaction, practice deep listening. Be fully present, and make sure the other person feels heard and valued.

---

[31] Davies, Rachel. "Poverty and Interiority in Mother Teresa." *Theological Studies*, vol. 80, no. 4, 2019, pp. 847–868

4. Inspiring Action: The Art of Motivation

Influence isn't just about inspiring people to believe in your vision—it's about motivating them to act on that belief. Great leaders know how to take their beliefs and inspire others to take tangible steps toward their goals.

Example: Barack Obama inspired millions with his message of hope and change. His leadership wasn't just about words—it was about motivating people to act, to vote, to get involved, and to believe in a brighter future.

What We Can Learn:

- **Belief Turns into Action**: People don't follow leaders just because of their words. They follow because they feel inspired to take action.
- **Motivation is about Purpose**: Motivation is most powerful when it's connected to a greater purpose. Leaders who inspire action tie that action to a vision of impact.

Actionable Tip: When you lead, always connect the why with the how. Help others understand how their actions contribute to the bigger picture.

5. Building a Movement: Leadership Beyond the Individual

True influence goes beyond one person's efforts. To build a lasting impact, you must empower others to take ownership of your vision and spread it. This is how movements are born. When your belief system resonates deeply enough, it has the power to spread like wildfire.

Example: Martin Luther King Jr. didn't just lead a movement by himself; he empowered others to become leaders, too. His belief in equality and justice became the foundation for a nationwide movement that transcended his individual efforts.

What We Can Learn:

- **Empower Others to Lead**: If you want to build a movement, you must create leaders, not followers. Empower people to live your belief and to spread it further than you ever could on your own.
- **Create a Legacy**: Great leaders don't just lead—they build a movement that lasts beyond their own lifetime.

Actionable Tip: Identify someone you can mentor or empower today. Share your belief, and give them the tools and resources to lead their own way.

The Three Key Elements of Mastering Influence:

1. **Vision**: Have a clear, compelling vision that people can rally behind.
2. **Empathy**: Build trust and connection by understanding others' needs.
3. **Action**: Motivate others to act on your belief, and empower them to become leaders in their own right.

3 The Three Key Elements of Mastering Influence:

Your Challenge: Become an Influencer of Change

Now that you understand the principles of influence, it's time to put them into action. How will you take your belief and inspire others? How will you empower people to take action and build a movement around your vision?

Your Takeaway:

True influence is not about manipulation—it's about leading with authenticity, empathy, and a clear purpose. When you inspire others to act, you are creating a ripple effect that can change the world.

Next: Chapter 10 – The Ripple Effect: How Your Belief Changes the World

In the next chapter, we'll dive into the ripple effect—how even the smallest actions, when rooted in belief, can create monumental change. Stay tuned.

Chapter 10

The Ripple Effect: How Your Belief Changes the World

Every great leader, innovator, and change-maker has understood the profound truth that beliefs, when acted upon, have the power to spark a ripple effect—a small action that creates far-reaching consequences, reverberating through people, communities, and even generations. Belief is not a static force; it is a dynamic, transformative energy that can spread and grow, touching lives in ways we often cannot predict or control.[32]

In this chapter, we'll explore how the ripple effect works, how one person's belief can change the course of history, and how you can harness that power to create lasting change in your own life and the world around you.

The Concept of the Ripple Effect

Imagine a single stone dropped into a calm pond. At first, there is only a small splash, but quickly, ripples begin to form, spreading outward and expanding further than the stone ever touched. This is the power of belief in motion—when you act on your beliefs, they begin to influence and inspire those around you, who, in turn, inspire others, and so on.[33]

The ripples of influence can multiply over time, creating waves of change. But to create this effect, it requires conviction, consistency, and action. Your belief must be grounded in something that compels you to act—and act in a way that aligns with your purpose.

---

[32] Ramstead, M. T. U., et al. "The Nature of Beliefs and Believing." *Frontiers in Psychology*, vol. 13, 2022, article 981925, https://doi.org/10.3389/fpsyg.2022.981925.

[33] Harper, Steve. "The Ripple Effect." *Maximizing the Power of Relationships for Your Life and Business* (2009): 2005.

Example: Malala Yousafzai's belief in education for girls changed the world. Her story started with a small act of defiance, standing up for her right to an education in the face of oppression. Her actions sparked an international movement for girls' education, influencing millions of people around the world to take action in their own communities.

What We Can Learn:

- **Belief is a Catalyst for Change**: Even a single act rooted in belief can have far-reaching consequences.
- **The Ripple Effect is Cumulative**: Each person who is touched by your belief has the potential to touch others, creating a growing wave of impact.

<u>Actionable Tip</u>: Think about one small action you can take today that reflects your deepest belief. Do it with full commitment and observe the ripple effects it creates.

The Power of Collective Belief: Building Communities of Change

As you begin to understand the power of the ripple effect, it's important to recognize that beliefs are not isolated. When individuals come together around a shared belief, the impact can be magnified exponentially. The collective power of a group united by a common vision is unstoppable.

Example: The Civil Rights Movement in the U.S. was driven by a collective belief in racial equality.[34] Leaders like Dr. Martin Luther King Jr. galvanized millions of people who shared that

---

[34] Chong, Dennis. *Collective action and the civil rights movement.* University of Chicago Press, 2014.

belief, creating a movement that resulted in legislative change and a shift in societal attitudes toward race and justice.

What We Can Learn:

- **Strength in Numbers**: When your belief resonates with others, it forms the foundation for collective action.
- **Movements Are Born from Shared Beliefs**: Change is most powerful when people come together, united by the same vision.

Actionable Tip: Find a community or group that shares your core belief. Work together to amplify your impact and create a movement that leads to real change.

The Role of Small Actions in Creating Big Impact

Many people believe that to make a difference, you need to take grand, sweeping actions. But in reality, it's the small, consistent actions that create the greatest change over time. Every small step you take to align with your beliefs contributes to the larger picture—the ripple effect that grows and spreads.

Example: Gandhi's Salt March was a simple, symbolic act—walking to the sea to make salt in defiance of British colonial laws. Yet it became a turning point in the Indian independence movement. It wasn't just the act itself but the idea behind it that inspired millions to take action and challenge oppressive systems.

What We Can Learn:

- **Small Acts Lead to Big Results**: Even the smallest action can have a profound ripple effect.

- **Consistency Builds Momentum**: Change doesn't happen overnight, but small, consistent actions compound over time to create significant impact.

Actionable Tip: Identify a small action you can take each day that reflects your beliefs. Over time, these small actions will create momentum and contribute to larger change.

How Beliefs Can Transform Individuals and Societies

Beliefs don't just affect your immediate surroundings—they have the power to transform entire societies. A deeply held belief can challenge existing norms, break down barriers, and reshape the cultural landscape.

Example: Nelson Mandela's belief in reconciliation and forgiveness helped dismantle apartheid in South Africa.[35] His journey from prisoner to president wasn't just a personal transformation; it was the transformation of an entire nation. His belief in unity and equality helped to heal a deeply divided society.

What We Can Learn:

- **Belief Shapes Societal Change**: One person's belief can inspire a shift in societal values and practices.

---

[35] Arslan, Havva Kök, and Yunus Turhan. "Reconciliation-oriented leadership: Nelson mandela and south africa." *All Azimuth: A Journal of Foreign Policy and Peace* 5.2 (2016): 29-46.

- **Transformation is a Collective Process**: While an individual's belief may spark the change, it takes the collective effort of many to sustain it.

Actionable Tip: Consider how your personal beliefs can contribute to larger societal issues. How can you use your influence to inspire broader change?

The Legacy of Belief: Leaving Your Mark on the World

The ripple effect doesn't end when you leave this world. When you act on your beliefs, you create a legacy—a legacy that can inspire future generations to continue the work you started. Your beliefs, rooted in actions and integrity, have the power to outlast your time here, influencing people long after you are gone.

Example: Mother Teresa's belief in serving the poorest of the poor continues to inspire countless individuals and organizations around the world. Her life was a testament to the power of belief to create a lasting legacy of compassion and service.

What We Can Learn:

- **Your Beliefs Create a Lasting Impact**: The actions you take today can inspire those who come after you to continue your work and beliefs.
- **Legacy is Built Through Service**: The greatest legacy comes from how you use your beliefs to serve others and create a better world.

Actionable Tip: Think about the kind of legacy you want to leave behind. What beliefs are you willing to dedicate your life to in order to create that impact?

Your Challenge: Create Your Ripple Effect

Now that you understand the power of the ripple effect, it's time to make it real in your own life. Every belief you hold, every action you take, every person you inspire—all of it contributes to a larger change. The question is: How will you create your own ripple effect?

Your Takeaway:

Your belief, no matter how small or large, can spark a chain of events that changes the world. Don't underestimate the power of your actions. Start small, act with conviction, and watch your belief grow into a movement.

Next: Chapter 11 – The Power of Persistence: How to Keep Believing When the World Doubts You

In the next chapter, we'll explore persistence—how to keep believing in yourself and your vision when faced with doubt, failure, and obstacles. Stay tuned.

Chapter 11

The Power of Persistence: How to Keep Believing When the World Doubts You

Belief alone is not enough. The true power of belief lies in persistence—the unwavering commitment to continue moving forward despite the obstacles, setbacks, and doubts that will inevitably arise along the way. Persistence is the quality that separates those who achieve their dreams from those who give up before they reach the finish line.

In this chapter, we will explore how persistence fuels the journey of turning your belief into action, and how it helps you overcome challenges and maintain momentum when the world seems to be against you.

Understanding the Role of Persistence in Achieving Big Goals

Every monumental achievement in history—whether personal, professional, or societal—has been achieved through the combination of belief and persistence.[36] Persistence is the bridge that connects where you are now to where you want to be. It's what keeps you going when the going gets tough and gives you the courage to keep moving forward even when the end goal seems distant.

Example: Thomas Edison is famous for inventing the light bulb. What many don't know is that he failed over 1,000 times before finally succeeding. When asked about his repeated failures, Edison replied, "I have not failed. I've just found 1,000

---

[36] Wu, Sibin, Matthews, and Grace K. Dagher. "Need for achievement, business goals, and entrepreneurial persistence." *Management Research News* 30.12 (2007): 928-941.

ways that won't work." His persistence in the face of failure was the key to his eventual success.[37]

What We Can Learn:

- **Failure is a Stepping Stone**: Persistence means learning from failures, adjusting, and continuing your journey without giving up.
- **Great Achievements Take Time**: Big goals often require consistent effort over time, even when results aren't immediately visible.

Actionable Tip: When facing a challenge, remind yourself that failure is part of the process. Reframe setbacks as opportunities to learn, and keep pushing forward.

The Psychology of Persistence: Why Some People Keep Going While Others Quit

Why do some people persist while others quit? The answer often lies in mindset. Those who persist have developed a growth mindset[38]—a belief that their abilities can be developed through hard work and dedication. In contrast, those who quit tend to have a fixed mindset, believing their capabilities are limited.

---

[37] Dyer, Frank Lewis, and Thomas Commerford Martin. *Edison: His Life and Inventions*. 2nd ed., vol. 2, Harper & Brothers, 1910, pp. 615–616.

[38] Dweck, Carol. "What having a "growth mindset" actually means." *Harvard business review* 13.2 (2016): 2-5.

Example: J.K. Rowling, the author of the Harry Potter series, was rejected by 12 publishers before finally being accepted by one. If she had quit after her first rejection, the world would never have known Harry Potter. But her belief in her work, paired with her persistence, led to one of the most successful book franchises in history.

What We Can Learn:

- **Mindset is Key**: A growth mindset helps you embrace challenges and setbacks as opportunities for growth, not signs to quit.
- **Resilience Comes from Belief**: The stronger your belief in your purpose, the more persistent you will be in the face of adversity.

<u>Actionable Tip</u>: Practice cultivating a growth mindset by embracing challenges, focusing on effort rather than outcomes, and viewing failures as opportunities for improvement.

Staying Persistent in the Face of Doubt and Criticism

Doubt is one of the biggest obstacles to persistence. When the world doubts you, it's easy to start doubting yourself. Self-doubt can undermine your belief, making it harder to persist. But remember, doubt is a natural part of the journey—what matters is how you respond to it.

Example: Walt Disney faced repeated criticism early in his career.[39] He was told he lacked creativity, and his first animation company went bankrupt. Yet Disney persisted. He continued to pursue his dream of creating an entertainment empire, despite the doubters. Today, Disney is a global brand that continues to influence entertainment worldwide.

What We Can Learn:

- **Doubt Is Universal**: Everyone experiences doubt, but the key to success is how you overcome it.
- **Persist Despite the Critics**: The opinions of others do not define your potential. Keep your focus on your vision, and let your actions speak louder than words.

Actionable Tip: When you face criticism or doubt, use it as fuel to prove others wrong. Focus on your vision, not on the negativity.

Building a Persistent Routine: Small Daily Actions Lead to Big Results

Persistence is not about doing everything at once. It's about taking small, consistent steps every day that align with your beliefs. Over time, these small actions compound to create significant change. The key to persistence is creating a routine—a daily practice that keeps you moving forward.

---

[39] Barrier, Michael. *The animated man: A life of Walt Disney.* Univ of California Press, 2007.

Example: Stephen King, one of the most successful authors of our time, wrote 2,000 words every day, even when he wasn't feeling inspired. His persistence in his daily writing routine led to the creation of some of the most iconic stories in literature.

What We Can Learn:

- **Daily Actions Build Momentum**: By committing to small, consistent actions, you create momentum that propels you toward your larger goals.
- **Routine Keeps You Focused**: A set routine helps you stay focused on what matters, even when distractions or doubts arise.

Actionable Tip: Set aside time each day to take at least one small action that moves you closer to your goal. Stick to this routine, even on days when motivation is low.

How to Keep Believing When Everyone Else is Giving Up

There will be times when it feels like everyone around you is giving up—when you feel like you're the only one still believing in your dream. It's in these moments that your belief and persistence will be tested. But remember, some of the world's greatest achievements have come from individuals who refused to give up when everyone else did.

Example: Oprah Winfrey was fired from her first television job because she was deemed "unfit for TV." But she didn't give up on her belief in her ability to connect with people and tell meaningful stories. Today, Oprah is a global icon and a media mogul, and her story is a testament to the power of persistence.

What We Can Learn:

- **Belief Is the Fuel for Persistence**: If you truly believe in your vision, you'll find the strength to persist even when others give up.
- **Persistence Requires Courage**: It takes courage to continue when everyone else has lost faith. But those who persist are often the ones who change the world.

Actionable Tip: When everyone else is quitting, remind yourself of your "why." Connect with your deeper purpose to find the courage to keep going.

The Legacy of Persistence: Leaving a Lasting Impact

Persistence doesn't just help you achieve your goals—it also creates a legacy that can inspire others long after you've achieved your dreams. By staying persistent, you not only shape your own future but also inspire others to pursue their beliefs and dreams, creating a ripple effect of perseverance and success.

Example: Martin Luther King Jr., despite facing violence, jail time, and countless obstacles, stayed persistent in his belief that nonviolent resistance could bring about social change. His persistence not only changed the course of American history but also inspired countless individuals around the world to fight for justice and equality.

What We Can Learn:

- **Persistence Leaves a Legacy**: Your commitment to your beliefs and goals can inspire future generations to follow in your footsteps.
- **Your Impact Lives On**: The effect of your persistence will continue to ripple out, influencing others even after you're gone.

Actionable Tip: As you persist in your goals, think about the legacy you want to leave behind. What will your persistence inspire in others?

Your Challenge: Stay Persistent, No Matter the Obstacle

In this chapter, we've explored how persistence is the secret weapon that will help you achieve your dreams. Now it's time to put it into practice. What belief do you hold most dear? What action can you take every day to bring that belief to life? And how will you stay persistent, no matter the obstacles that stand in your way?

Your Takeaway:

Persistence is the key to turning belief into reality. It requires consistent action, even in the face of doubt, criticism, and setbacks. If you stay persistent, there is no limit to what you can achieve.

Next: Chapter 12 – Belief and Leadership: Inspiring Others to Follow Your Vision

In the next chapter, we will delve into the connection between belief and leadership. We'll explore how your belief can inspire others, rally them to your cause, and help you create a movement that impacts the world. Stay tuned!

Chapter 12

Belief and Leadership: Inspiring Others to Follow Your Vision

Leadership is not just about being in charge; it's about inspiring and guiding others toward a common vision.[40] When you hold a powerful belief, it has the potential to influence, uplift, and motivate those around you. Belief-driven leadership is the ability to transform a vision into reality by convincing others to believe in that vision and take action together.

In this chapter, we will explore how belief shapes leadership, how leaders inspire others, and how you can harness the power of belief to become a leader who not only achieves success but also leaves a lasting impact on the world.

The Essence of Belief-Driven Leadership

At the core of effective leadership is belief—the unshakable conviction in your vision, purpose, and mission. When leaders believe in their cause, they can engage and inspire others to believe in it as well. Leadership rooted in belief has the power to rally people to action, overcome adversity, and create meaningful change.[41]

Example: Nelson Mandela is one of the most revered leaders of the 20th century, largely because of his unwavering belief in equality and justice for all. His belief in a free, democratic South Africa inspired millions to follow his lead, despite decades of systemic oppression. His leadership was not just about strategy; it was about belief in the possibility of a better future.

---

[40] Conger, Jay A. "Inspiring others: The language of leadership." *Academy of Management Perspectives* 5.1 (1991): 31-45.

[41] Sharma, Monica. *Radical transformational leadership: strategic action for change agents*. North Atlantic Books, 2017.

What We Can Learn:

- **Belief Drives Leadership**: Leaders who deeply believe in their mission can inspire others to take ownership and work toward a shared goal.
- **Authenticity Matters**: True leaders do not merely dictate—they embody their beliefs, making them magnetic and powerful to others.

<u>Actionable Tip</u>: To lead effectively, take time to articulate your beliefs and vision clearly. Your belief should be your guiding force and be reflected in your actions, words, and decisions.

Inspiring Others with Your Vision: The Power of Conviction

One of the most powerful aspects of belief-driven leadership is the ability to inspire others. The best leaders do not force others to follow them—they inspire them through their vision, passion, and conviction. When you truly believe in your vision, your energy and passion will naturally attract others who share your values.

Example: Steve Jobs was known for his ability to inspire his team at Apple with his vision for innovation and design excellence. Jobs didn't just create products; he created a belief system around the company's mission to "think different." His belief in pushing the boundaries of technology and design was contagious and helped create one of the most successful companies in history.

What We Can Learn:

- **Conviction Is Contagious**: When you believe in your vision, you ignite that same belief in others.
- **Leaders Paint a Picture of the Future**: The most inspiring leaders help others see a vision of a better future and show them how they can be part of it.

Actionable Tip: Communicate your vision with passion. Be clear about what you believe in and why it matters. Share your vision in a way that resonates with others and motivates them to get on board.

Building Trust through Belief

Trust is the foundation of effective leadership.[42] When you believe in something deeply, it shows in your decisions, actions, and communication. Your belief becomes a beacon that guides you and those you lead. This transparency and conviction build trust, which is essential for creating a loyal and engaged team.

Example: Abraham Lincoln demonstrated remarkable leadership during one of America's most divisive periods—the Civil War.[43] Despite immense opposition, his belief in the Union and the abolition of slavery never wavered. His ability to communicate that belief with integrity and consistency earned

---

[42] Gordon, Gus. "Leadership through trust." *Springer Books* (2017).

[43] Iodice, Emilio F. "The leadership of Abraham Lincoln: Why it matters today." *The Journal of Values-Based Leadership* 15.2 (2022): 16.

him the trust of the American people and leaders alike, helping to navigate the nation through its most challenging times.

What We Can Learn:

- **Trust Is Built on Consistency**: When your actions align with your beliefs, you earn the trust of those around you.
- **Integrity Is Non-Negotiable**: Leaders who consistently act according to their beliefs build long-term trust and respect.

<u>**Actionable Tip**</u>: Always align your actions with your words. Live your beliefs and hold yourself accountable to the same standards you set for others.

Turning Obstacles into Opportunities: Resilience in Leadership

Leadership often requires navigating adversity and overcoming challenges. However, belief-driven leaders use challenges as opportunities to grow and strengthen their vision. Their belief in their cause helps them view obstacles not as roadblocks, but as opportunities to demonstrate resilience and creativity in solving problems.

Example: Mahatma Gandhi led India to independence with an unshakable belief in nonviolent resistance. Throughout his life, he faced immense obstacles—imprisonment, violence, and personal loss—but his belief in nonviolence and justice kept him focused. His ability to stay resilient in the face of hardship was a key element of his leadership, inspiring millions to join the movement.

What We Can Learn:

- **Resilience Comes from Belief**: Leaders who believe in their mission are better equipped to stay resilient in the face of setbacks.
- **Obstacles Are Opportunities for Growth**: When you face adversity, it's often an opportunity to innovate and improve your approach.

<u>**Actionable Tip**</u>: When faced with an obstacle, pause and reflect. Reconnect with your belief and vision, and ask yourself how you can turn this challenge into a learning experience.

The Role of Empathy and Compassion in Belief-Driven Leadership

Leadership is not just about achieving results—it's about guiding and supporting the people you lead. A belief-driven leader shows empathy[44] and compassion, understanding that the journey is just as important as the destination. The best leaders use their belief to create a supportive environment where others feel valued and empowered to reach their full potential.

Example: Mother Teresa led with an extraordinary sense of compassion and belief in serving the poor and sick. Her leadership was not about power or influence—it was about her deep belief in humanity and service to others. Through her acts

---

[44] Zivkovic, Sanja. "Empathy in leadership: how it enhances effectiveness." *Economic and Social Development: Book of Proceedings* (2022): 454-467.

of love and kindness, she inspired millions around the world to take action in their communities.

What We Can Learn:

- **Compassion is Central to Leadership**: Belief-driven leadership isn't just about directing people—it's about supporting and empowering them to grow.
- **Empathy Builds Stronger Connections**: When you lead with compassion, you create an environment where people feel safe to share their ideas and talents.

<u>**Actionable Tip**</u>: Show compassion in your leadership by listening actively, offering support, and empowering those around you to succeed.

Becoming the Leader You Were Meant to Be

Becoming a belief-driven leader requires more than just believing in a vision—it requires living that belief every day. It's about consistently showing up with passion, integrity, and resilience, and inspiring others to follow your example.

Your Leadership Challenge:

1. **Define Your Beliefs**: What do you believe in deeply? What are you willing to fight for?
2. **Inspire Others**: How can you communicate your vision in a way that inspires others to take action?
3. **Lead with Integrity**: Ensure that your actions align with your beliefs. Trust is earned through consistency.

4. **Stay Resilient**: When faced with obstacles, reconnect with your beliefs and use adversity as an opportunity for growth.

Your Takeaway:

Belief-driven leadership is a powerful force for change. When you align your beliefs with your actions, you inspire others to do the same, creating a movement that can change the world.

Next: Chapter 13 – The Ripple Effect: How Your Belief Can Impact the World

In the next chapter, we will explore the ripple effect of belief—how your actions and leadership can influence others and create a legacy of change. We'll dive into how small, belief-driven actions can lead to massive global impact, and how you can use your belief to leave the world better than you found it.

Stay tuned!

Chapter 13

The Ripple Effect: How Your Belief Can Impact the World

The power of belief extends far beyond the individual. While it can drive personal success and leadership, it also has the incredible potential to spark social change, movements, and legacies that reverberate through generations. Belief is a force that can transform the world, one person, one action at a time.

In this chapter, we will explore how a single belief can create a ripple effect—a cascade of influence that touches the lives of others and spreads across communities, nations, and the world. By understanding this ripple effect, you can leverage your belief to make an impact that transcends your immediate circle.

The Ripple Effect of Belief: A Catalyst for Change

Every belief, whether positive or negative, has a ripple effect.[45] Just as a stone dropped in water creates expanding waves, your belief can spread, inspire, and influence others far beyond your initial reach. The true power of belief lies not only in what you think or do but in how it affects those around you and continues to reverberate over time.

Example: Consider the life and work of Martin Luther King Jr., whose belief in equality, justice, and nonviolence sparked a movement that changed the course of American history. His message resonated with millions, and through peaceful protests, speeches, and activism, King's belief in civil rights inspired countless individuals to stand up for justice and equality[46], influencing not only the United States but the world.

---

[45] Lee, Jason Vaughn, and Annelise Marie Pietenpol. "The Ripple Effect."

[46] King, Richard H. *Civil rights and the idea of freedom.* University of Georgia Press, 1996.

What We Can Learn:

- **Belief is Contagious**: The beliefs you hold and the actions you take can inspire others to believe in the same cause.[47]
- **Small Actions Lead to Big Impact**: You don't have to change the world all at once. A single, well-intentioned action rooted in your belief can lead to a chain of events that create lasting change.

Actionable Tip: Recognize that every action you take based on your belief is a stone in the water. Start with one small act of kindness, inspiration, or leadership, and watch how it ripples out to others.

The Power of a Collective Belief: Movements and Social Change

When many individuals share the same belief and unite under a common cause, the ripple effect expands exponentially. Movements for social change are born when individuals with a shared belief come together to challenge systems, fight for justice, and advocate for a better future. These collective beliefs can alter societal norms[48], dismantle injustice, and create lasting transformation.

---

[47] Graeber, Thomas, Christopher Roth, and Constantin Schesch. *Contagious Beliefs*. Working Paper, 2023.

[48] Tschannen-Moran, Megan, Serena J. Salloum, and Roger D. Goddard. "Context matters: The influence of collective beliefs and shared norms." *International handbook of research on teachers' beliefs*. Routledge, 2014. 301-316.

Example: The #MeToo movement[49], which gained momentum in 2017, was a collective belief in the power of speaking out against sexual harassment and assault. What started as a hashtag on social media became a global movement, empowering millions of people—especially women—to share their stories and demand change. The ripple effect of this movement is still being felt today, as it continues to influence policies, workplaces, and societal norms.

What We Can Learn:

- **Collective Beliefs Drive Movements**: When many people share the same belief, they can unite to challenge systems and create significant social change.
- **Courage to Speak Out**: Change often begins with one voice, but it can grow into a movement when others are empowered to speak up as well.

Actionable Tip: Look for ways to join or create a community of like-minded individuals who share your beliefs. Together, you can amplify your efforts and create powerful change.

Legacy: How Belief Transcends Time

The impact of a belief doesn't stop with the individuals who hold it—it continues to transcend time through legacy. A strong belief can leave behind a blueprint for future generations to follow, helping to shape the world long after we are gone. Every

---

[49] Hillstrom, Laurie Collier. *The# metoo movement*. Bloomsbury Publishing USA, 2018.

leader, innovator, and activist who has ever made a lasting impact has done so by planting the seeds of belief in the world.

Example: Wright brothers, Orville and Wilbur Wright changed the course of history by believing that human flight was possible.[50] Their belief in the power of innovation and exploration led them to invent the airplane, a technology that transformed travel, commerce, and warfare. The impact of their belief lives on through the aerospace industry and the way we connect globally.

What We Can Learn:

- **Legacy is Built on Belief**: The most impactful legacies are formed when individuals channel their beliefs into actions that have lasting consequences.
- **Your Belief Can Shape Future Generations**: What you believe today can influence the way future generations think, act, and live.

Actionable Tip: Think about the legacy you want to leave. What beliefs and actions will you instill in others that will shape the future for the better?

Creating Positive Ripples in Your Daily Life

The beauty of the ripple effect is that it doesn't require grand gestures. The small actions we take every day can have a profound impact on others. Whether it's through acts of

---

[50] Howard, Fred. *Wilbur and Orville: a biography of the Wright brothers.* Courier Corporation, 2013.

kindness, empathy, or simply standing by our beliefs, we have the ability to create ripples that inspire and transform the world.

Example: Malala Yousafzai's belief in the right to education for all girls has inspired millions worldwide.[51] Despite facing violence and adversity, her commitment to her belief in education has led her to become a global advocate. Through her activism, she has empowered countless young girls to fight for their right to education.

What We Can Learn:

- **Even Small Acts Create Ripples**: You don't have to be a famous activist or leader to make an impact. Your everyday actions, rooted in belief, can inspire others.
- **Empathy and Compassion Create Positive Change**: When you lead with empathy and compassion, you inspire those around you to do the same.

Actionable Tip: Look for opportunities every day to create ripples. Whether it's a smile, a supportive word, or a helping hand, your actions can influence someone's day—and possibly their life.

The Global Ripple: Changing the World Through Collective Action

The ripple effect of belief is not limited to small actions or individual movements. It can expand globally, affecting entire

---

[51] Ikrama, Syeda, and Syeda Maseeha Qumer. "Malala Yousafzai: promoting girls' education in conflict-affected countries." *The Case For Women* (2023): 1-30.

nations and regions. When a belief takes hold across borders, it can lead to global change, influencing politics, economics, culture, and even the environment.

Example: Greta Thunberg[52], the climate activist from Sweden, has become a global symbol for youth-led environmental activism. Her belief in the urgency of addressing climate change has inspired millions of young people worldwide to take action. Through her speeches, protests, and advocacy, Thunberg has brought the climate crisis to the forefront of global discussions, urging leaders to act for the planet's future.[53]

What We Can Learn:

- **Global Change Begins with Belief**: The most profound global movements start with a shared belief that drives collective action across borders.
- **Young People Are Driving Change**: The belief-driven activism of young people is reshaping global conversations and inspiring change in every corner of the world.

<u>Actionable Tip</u>: Consider how you can align your beliefs with global issues and contribute to larger-scale solutions. Join or start global initiatives, and amplify the ripple effect of your beliefs.

---

[52] Thunberg, Greta. *No one is too small to make a difference*. Penguin, 2019.

[53] Thunberg, Greta. *The climate book: The facts and the solutions*. Penguin, 2024.

Turning Your Beliefs into Global Action

The ripple effect of belief starts small but can grow into something far greater. To truly impact the world, you must be intentional about channeling your beliefs into action. Whether it's through leadership, community engagement, or global advocacy, your belief can drive significant change.

Your Challenge:

- **Identify the Beliefs That Matter Most to You**: What do you believe in deeply? What causes do you feel passionate about?
- **Start Small**: Remember, even small actions rooted in belief can create a ripple effect.
- **Take Action for the Greater Good**: How can you contribute to creating a positive ripple in your community, country, or world?
- **Create a Legacy**: Think about how your beliefs can transcend time and create lasting change for future generations.

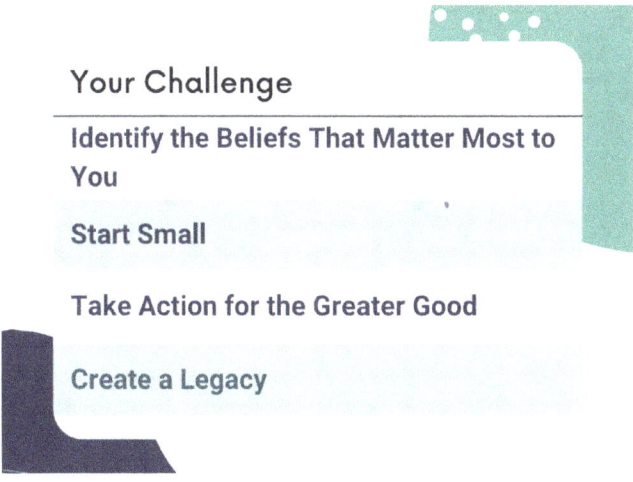

Your Challenge

Identify the Beliefs That Matter Most to You

Start Small

Take Action for the Greater Good

Create a Legacy

Next: Chapter 14 – Conclusion: The Power of Belief to Transform Your Life and the World

In the final chapter, we will bring together everything we've discussed and explore how you can harness the power of belief to create a life of purpose, success, and impact. It's time to step into your power, own your beliefs, and use them to leave a lasting mark on the world.

Stay tuned!

Conclusion

Chapter 14

Harnessing the Power of Belief to Transform Your Life and the World

As we reach the conclusion of this transformative journey into the power of belief, it is important to reflect on how far you've come and the limitless potential that lies ahead. Your beliefs are not just ideas—they are the foundation of your actions, the source of your strength, and the driving force that can shape your destiny.

In this final chapter, we will distill everything we have learned and explore how to harness the transformative power of belief to make an indelible impact on your life, your community, and the world.

The Power of Belief: A Personal Journey

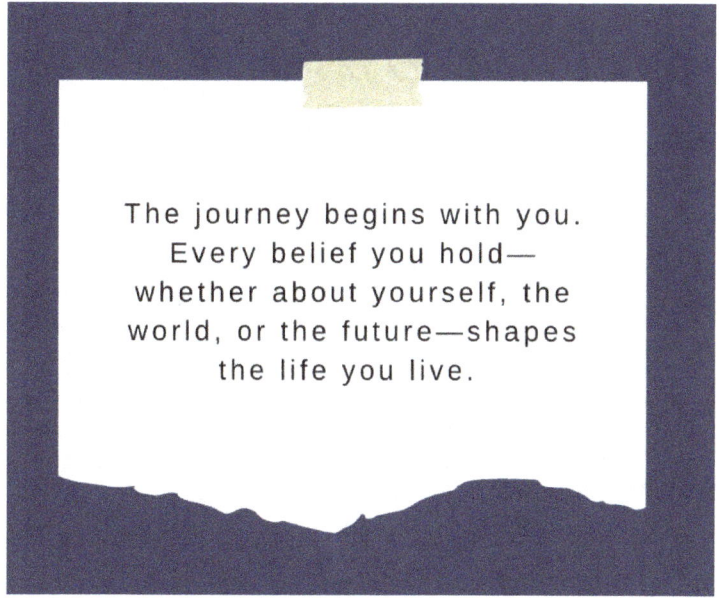

The journey begins with you.
Every belief you hold—
whether about yourself, the
world, or the future—shapes
the life you live.

Belief is the lens through which we perceive the world, and it influences how we act, react, and interact with others. When we intentionally shape and reinforce empowering beliefs, we are setting the stage for personal transformation.

Reflection: Take a moment to think about the beliefs that have shaped your life thus far. Are they beliefs that empower and uplift you? Or are they limiting beliefs that have held you back? Your first step is to examine your beliefs, challenge the ones that no longer serve you, and replace them with beliefs that align with your goals and aspirations.

<u>Actionable Tip</u>: To transform your life, begin by identifying and challenging limiting beliefs. Replace them with empowering beliefs that reflect your potential, such as "I am capable," "I have the power to change," or "My actions matter."

Belief as the Blueprint for Your Success

Belief acts as the blueprint for success—when you believe in your potential, you unlock your ability to achieve greatness. Every successful person, from innovators to activists, has one thing in common: a steadfast belief in their mission and their capacity to make a difference. This belief is not static; it grows and evolves through action, experience, and perseverance.

Example: Consider the success stories of people like Steve Jobs, whose belief in the power of innovation led to the creation of Apple, or Oprah Winfrey, whose belief in her own worth transformed her from an underprivileged child to a global media mogul. Both individuals faced adversity, but their belief in themselves and their purpose propelled them toward success.

What We Can Learn:

- **Belief Drives Action**: The more you believe in your ability to succeed, the more motivated you become to take consistent action.

- **Failure is Part of the Process**: Belief doesn't mean that challenges won't arise; rather, it means that you trust in your ability to overcome them.

Actionable Tip: Set clear, measurable goals and take small steps toward them every day. Strengthen your belief by seeing the results of your actions and progress.

Belief as the Foundation of Leadership

True leadership is rooted in belief. The most influential leaders throughout history have been those who believed not just in their own abilities, but in the abilities of others. They understood that empowering others to share in their vision was essential to creating lasting change.

Example: Nelson Mandela, whose belief in racial equality and peace led him to endure 27 years in prison, ultimately united South Africa. His ability to lead others through a shared belief in justice and unity changed the course of an entire nation.

What We Can Learn:

- **Belief Creates Leaders**: Leadership is not about authority; it's about inspiring others through your belief in a cause, a mission, or a shared goal.
- **Empowerment is Key**: True leaders build belief in others, helping them realize their own potential.

Actionable Tip: Lead by example. Share your beliefs openly, support others in their personal growth, and empower them to take action toward collective goals.

Turning Belief into Impact: Making Your Mark on the World

The true power of belief lies in its ability to create a lasting impact. Whether you are striving for personal success or working to create social change, your belief will be the driving force behind the impact you make. From small actions to global movements, belief is the foundation of change.

Example: Malala Yousafzai's belief in the right to education for girls has touched millions of lives. What started as a singular belief has grown into a global movement that continues to inspire educational reform worldwide. Her story proves that even one voice, driven by unwavering belief, can create monumental change.

What We Can Learn:

- **Small Actions Can Lead to Global Change**: Every positive belief can lead to a ripple effect that extends far beyond your own life.
- **Your Legacy is Built on Belief**: The impact you make through your beliefs can live on long after you are gone.

Actionable Tip: Identify a cause or issue you are deeply passionate about, and use your belief to take action. Whether through advocacy, community service, or leadership, let your beliefs guide your efforts to create positive change.

Transforming the World with Belief: Global Impact

The power of belief extends beyond the individual, transcending borders, cultures, and nations. When collective belief aligns with a shared purpose, it becomes a force capable of reshaping the world. Global movements, revolutions, and cultural shifts are all products of belief, harnessed and amplified by groups of people united in their vision for a better future.

Example: The civil rights movement in the United States was built on the belief that all people, regardless of race, should be treated equally. This belief ignited a movement that ultimately resulted in significant legislative and cultural changes, not just in America but around the world.

What We Can Learn:

- **Global Movements Begin with Belief**: When like-minded individuals unite behind a shared belief, they can create social, political, and economic changes on a global scale.
- **Belief Transforms Societies**: Large-scale change begins with a shift in collective belief, which leads to collective action.

Actionable Tip: Join or create movements that align with your values and beliefs. Together, you can make a global impact.

Conclusion: Your Belief, Your Legacy

As you embark on your journey of transformation, remember that your belief is your greatest asset. It will guide you through challenges, fuel your passion, and empower you to create the life and world you desire. By cultivating empowering beliefs and using them to fuel your actions, you will create a legacy that is meaningful, lasting, and transformative.

You have the power to shape your destiny, and in doing so, you can leave the world better than you found it. The key is to understand the power of belief—not just as an idea, but as a tool for action, leadership, and change.

Your Challenge: Start today. Identify your core beliefs, refine them, and use them to fuel your personal transformation. Take bold action, inspire others, and make your mark on the world. Your belief can change everything.

Epilogue

The Power of Belief Is Yours to Harness

The journey you've begun does not end here. As you continue to grow, learn, and take action, remember that belief is a lifelong practice. It is a force that is ever-evolving, shaping your thoughts, actions, and outcomes. Embrace it, nurture it, and watch as it propels you to new heights of success, fulfillment, and impact.

— 66 —————————

Your belief is the most powerful tool you have. Use it wisely, and the world will follow.

————————— 99 —

Thank you for joining this journey into the power of belief. May your belief lead you to greatness and inspire you to leave a lasting impact on the world.

Recommended Reading

To deepen your understanding of belief and its power to shape lives, movements, and the world, we recommend the following foundational works. These books have informed our thinking and complement the themes explored throughout this volume.

On Belief and Mindset

- Mindset: The New Psychology of Success by Carol S. Dweck
- The Biology of Belief by Bruce H. Lipton
- The Power of Now by Eckhart Tolle
- Learned Optimism by Martin Seligman

On Influence and Leadership

- Start with Why by Simon Sinek
- Leaders Eat Last by Simon Sinek
- The Art of War by Sun Tzu
- Good to Great by Jim Collins

On Mass Movements and Social Change

- Rules for Radicals by Saul D. Alinsky
- The True Believer by Eric Hoffer
- Why Nations Fail by Daron Acemoglu & James A. Robinson
- The Structure of Scientific Revolutions by Thomas S. Kuhn

On Identity, Psychology, and Transformation

- The Untethered Soul by Michael A. Singer
- Man's Search for Meaning by Viktor E. Frankl
- Atomic Habits by James Clear
- The Four Agreements by Don Miguel Ruiz

Appendix

Tools, Exercises, and Frameworks

This appendix contains a selection of practical tools referenced throughout the book, designed to help you actively implement the power of belief in your life and leadership.

1. The Belief Audit

- Identify current core beliefs
- Categorize as empowering or limiting
- Rewrite limiting beliefs in empowering terms
- Use daily affirmations to reinforce new beliefs

2. The Belief-to-Action Blueprint

- Belief → Emotion → Action → Result
- Reflect on beliefs behind current habits
- Choose a new belief, act on it, track outcomes

3. The Ripple Reflection

- Who influenced your beliefs?
- Whose beliefs have you influenced?
- How can you intentionally use your belief to create impact?

4. The Influence Map

- Identify 5 people you want to inspire
- Define the belief you want to transfer
- Create a strategy for communicating, modeling, and reinforcing that belief

5. Daily Belief Ritual

- Morning: Repeat your core belief aloud (ex: "I create meaningful impact through what I believe")
- Midday: One small action that affirms this belief
- Evening: Reflect—How did I embody this belief today?

Resources by the Authors

Books, Courses, and Materials by Mardoche Sidor, M.D., Karen Dubin, Ph.D., LCSW, and the SWEET Institute

The following books and resources expand on the themes in this book, offering deeper dives into leadership, psychology, mental wellness, and transformational learning.

Books by the SWEET Institute

- Journey to Empowerment
- Discovering Your Worth: Everything You Need to Feel Fulfilled
- The Power of Faith: A Harvard-Trained Psychiatrist Speaking on Faith
- The Psychotherapy Certificate Course: The Clinician and Coach Manual (Books 1–3)
- The Anxiety Course: The Workbook
- What's Missing
- NLP for Clinicians

Select Publications and Articles via the SWEET Institute

- How to Connect Effectively in Relationships: Building Meaningful Bonds
- Recognizing Patterns in Behaviors in Relationships
- The Courage to Do: Embracing Action in the Face of Fear
- Babur's Legacy: Resilience and Adaptability in Mental Well-Being
- Why the SWEET Institute Starts Its Mission with Social Work

Courses and Trainings

The SWEET Institute offers dozens of CE-accredited trainings and certificate programs for clinicians, leaders, and change-makers, including:

- Motivational Interviewing Certificate Course
- Advanced Narrative Therapy
- Gestalt Therapy for Experienced Professionals
- Transference-Focused Psychotherapy Series
- Psychedelics in Clinical Practice
- Leadership for Clinicians

For more information or to join upcoming seminars and communities of learning:

Visit www.sweetinstitute.com

www.ingramcontent.com/pod-product-compliance
Lightning Source LLC
Chambersburg PA
CBHW071156120626
46546CB00006B/2296